Torture

Lisa Hajjar

D0060883

Torture is indisputably abhorrent. Why, you might ask, would you even want to think or read about torture? That is a very good question, and one this book addresses in a compelling and enlightening way. Torture is a very important issue, not least because millions of people around the world have been subjected to this odious practice, and many are enduring torture right now as you read these words.

Lisa Hajjar is Associate Professor of Sociology at the University of California, Santa Barbara.

University Readers
Reading Materials Evolved.

THE SOCIAL ISSUES
COLLECTION™

Routledge
Taylor & Francis Group

Framing 21st Century Social Issues

The goal of this new, unique Series is to offer readable, teachable "thinking frames" on today's social problems and social issues by leading scholars. These are available for view on http://routledge.custom-gateway.com/routledge-social-issues.html.

For instructors teaching a wide range of courses in the social sciences, the Routledge *Social Issues Collection* now offers the best of both worlds: originally written short texts that provide "overviews" to important social issues *as well as* teachable excerpts from larger works previously published by Routledge and other presses.

As an instructor, click to the website to view the library and decide how to build your custom anthology and which thinking frames to assign. Students can choose to receive the assigned materials in print and/or electronic formats at an affordable price.

Available

Terror: Social, Political, and Economic Perspectives
Marl Worrell

Body Problems
Running and Living Long in a Fast-Food Society
Ben Agger

Sex, Drugs, and Death
Addressing Youth Problems in American Society
Tammy Anderson

The Stupidity Epidemic
Worrying about Students, Schools, and America's Future
Joel Best

Empire versus Democracy
The Triumph of Corporate and Military Power
Carl Boggs

Contentious Identities
Ethnic, Religious, and Nationalist Conflicts in Today's World
Daniel Chirot

The Future of Higher Education
Dan Clawson and Max Page

Waste and Consumption
Capitalism, the Environment, and the Life of Things
Simonetta Falasca-Zamponi

Rapid Climate Change
Causes, Consequences, and Solutions
Scott G. McNall

The Problem of Emotions in Societies
Jonathan H. Turner

Outsourcing the Womb
Race, Class, and Gestational Surrogacy in a Global Market
France Winddance Twine

Changing Times for Black Professionals
Adia Harvey Wingfield

Why Nations Go to War
A Sociology of Military Conflict
Mark P. Worrell

How Ethical Systems Change: Eugenics, the Final Solution, Bioethics
Sheldon Ekland-Olson and Julie Beicken

How Ethical Systems Change: Abortion and Neonatal Care
Sheldon Ekland-Olson and Elyshia Aseltine

How Ethical Systems Change: Tolerable Suffering and Assisted Dying
Sheldon Ekland-Olson and Elyshia Aseltine

How Ethical Systems Change: Lynching and Capital Punishment
Sheldon Ekland-Olson and Danielle Dirks

Nuclear Family Values, Extended Family Lives
The Power of Race, Class, and Gender
Natalia Sarkisian and Naomi Gerstel

Disposable Youth, Racialized Memories, and the Culture of Cruelty
Henry Giroux

Due Process Denied: Detentions and Deportations in the United States
Tanya Golash-Boza

Oversharing: Presentation of Self in the Internet Age
Ben Agger

Foreign Remedies: What the Experience of Other Nations Can Tell Us about Next Steps in Reforming U.S. Health Care
David A. Rochefort and Kevin P. Donnelly

DIY: The Search for Control and Self-Reliance in the 21st Century
Kevin Wehr

Forthcoming

Are We Coddling Prisoners?
Benjamin Fleury-Steiner

Identity Problems in the Facebook Era
Daniel Trottier

Trafficking and Terror
Pardis Mahdavi

Beyond the Prison Industrial Complex
Kevin Wehr and Elyshia Aseltine

Color Line?
Krystal Beamon

Is Working Longer the Answer?
Tay McNamara and John Williamson

iTime
Ben Agger

Torture
A Sociology of Violence and Human Rights

Lisa Hajjar

University of California, Santa Barbara

Routledge
Taylor & Francis Group

NEW YORK AND LONDON

First published 2013
by Routledge
711 Third Avenue, New York, NY 10017

Simultaneously published in the UK
by Routledge
2 Park Square, Milton Park, Abingdon, Oxon OX14 4RN

Routledge is an imprint of the Taylor & Francis Group, an informa business

© 2013 Taylor & Francis

Library of Congress Cataloging-in-Publication Data
Hajjar, Lisa, 1961-Torture : a sociology of violence and human rights / Lisa Hajjar.
    p. cm. — (Framing 21st century social issues)
Includes bibliographical references and index.
ISBN 978-0-415-51806-2 (pbk. : alk. paper) — ISBN 978-0-203-12355-3
(ebook : alk. paper) 1. Torture—History. 2. Human rights—History. I. Title.
HV8593.H313 2013
364.6'7—dc23   2012026398

ISBN: 978-0-415-51806-2 (pbk)
ISBN: 978-0-203-12355-3 (ebk)

Typeset in Garamond and Gill Sans
by Cenveo Publisher Services

Contents

Series Foreword   ix

Preface   xi

  I: Why Are We (Still) Talking about Torture?   1

 II: Torture's Past   14

III: Modern Torture   21

 IV: Torture and Rights   33

  V: Enforcing the Right Not To Be Tortured   44

 VI: What's Wrong with Torture?   51

      References   62

      Glossary/Index   70

Series Foreword

The world in the early 21st century is beset with problems—a troubled economy, global warming, oil spills, religious and national conflict, poverty, HIV, health problems associated with sedentary lifestyles. Virtually no nation is exempt, and everyone, even in affluent countries, feels the impact of these global issues.

Since its inception in the 19th century, sociology has been the academic discipline dedicated to analyzing social problems. It is still so today. Sociologists offer not only diagnoses; they glimpse solutions, which they then offer to policy makers and citizens who work for a better world. Sociology played a major role in the civil rights movement during the 1960s in helping us to understand racial inequalities and prejudice, and it can play a major role today as we grapple with old and new issues.

This series builds on the giants of sociology, such as Weber, Durkheim, Marx, Parsons, and Mills. It uses their frames, and newer ones, to focus on particular issues of contemporary concern. These books are about the nuts and bolts of social problems, but they are equally about the frames through which we analyze these problems. It is clear by now that there is no single correct way to view the world, but only paradigms, models, which function as lenses through which we peer. For example, in analyzing oil spills and environmental pollution, we can use a frame that views such outcomes as unfortunate results of a reasonable effort to harvest fossil fuels. "Drill, baby, drill" sometimes involves certain costs as pipelines rupture and oil spews forth. Or we could analyze these environmental crises as inevitable outcomes of our effort to dominate nature in the interest of profit. The first frame would solve oil spills with better environmental protection measures and clean-ups, while the second frame would attempt to prevent them altogether, perhaps shifting away from the use of petroleum and natural gas and toward alternative energies that are "green."

These books introduce various frames such as these for viewing social problems. They also highlight debates between social scientists who frame problems differently. The books suggest solutions, both on the macro and micro levels. That is, they suggest what new policies might entail, and they also identify ways in which people, from the ground level, can work toward a better world, changing themselves and their lives and families and providing models of change for others.

Readers do not need an extensive background in academic sociology to benefit from these books. Each book is student-friendly in that we provide glossaries of terms for the uninitiated that are keyed to bolded terms in the text. Each chapter ends with questions for further thought and discussion. The level of each book is accessible to undergraduate students, even as these books offer sophisticated and innovative analyses.

This is the third year of our Routledge social-issues book series. These brief books explore key contemporary social problems in ways that introduce basic concepts in the social sciences, cover key literature in the field, and offer original analyses and diagnoses. Our series includes books on topics ranging widely from global warming, to global ethnic conflict, to comparative health care, to oversharing on the Internet. These readable treatments can be assigned in both lower- and upper-division sociology courses in which instructors seek affordable, pithy treatments of social problems.

Our series is framed by our increasingly global world in which economic inequalities produce political and military conflicts. Just as insurgents and governments use terror as a normal means of conducting political life, they also sometimes torture their enemies and captives. Here, Lisa Hajjar examines torture in her illuminating and disturbing book for this series.

Preface

Torture is indisputably abhorrent. The word brings to mind people having their fingernails extracted with pliers or electric shocks applied to their genitals. Why, you might ask, would you even want to think or read about torture? That is a very good question, and one this book will address, hopefully in a compelling and enlightening way. Torture is a very important issue, not least because millions of people around the world have been subjected to this odious practice—and many are enduring torture right now as you read these words.

But torture is important in other ways as well. Until the Age of Enlightenment, torture was a permitted and necessary feature of legal systems in continental Europe and some other parts of the world. Moves to abolish the reliance on torture as a tool of law enforcement, starting in the late 18th century, laid the foundations of modern legal liberalism that we appreciate or even take for granted today: the principles that people have rights and that a government should not brutalize and terrorize individuals who are in custody and have no capacity to defend themselves. Establishing a right not to be tortured coincided with the establishment of legal limits on the power of government, specifically depriving officials of any "right" to torture. The effects of these moves contributed to the creation of new norms of "good government," which have become the universal ideal. Although more than two-thirds of the world's governments still use torture, today we can condemn this as illegal and unacceptable.

The right not to be tortured is very strong in principle, but in practice that right is fragile like the bodies and psyches it targets. When states torture, even if they deny in public what they do in secret or euphemize what they do as "not torture," it affects us all. Why? You might be safe in the belief that *you* will never be tortured, and for the vast majority of you, that is true. But the reason the right not to be tortured is important to you and everyone else is because it is the most universal right that human beings have, matched only by the right not to be enslaved. Every person on earth has the right not to be tortured under all circumstances. You don't have to be a good person to have this right; you just have to be a person.

If that right is usurped or eroded by exceptions to the rule, for example the claimed necessity of torturing terrorists or foreign enemies, that means that states are (re) claiming the *right* to do whatever they want to whomever they want. The historical record shows that wherever torture gains a foothold, its use spreads. Why should you be interested in torture and perhaps even speak out against it? Consider the words of Pastor Martin Niemöller who criticized the complacency of many Germans following the Nazis' rise to power in the 1930s:

> First they came for the *communists*, and I didn't speak out because I wasn't a communist.
> Then they came for the *trade unionists*, and I didn't speak out because I wasn't a trade unionist.
> Then they came for the *Jews*, and I didn't speak out because I wasn't a Jew.
> Then they came for me and there was no one left to speak out for me.

In 2001, the U.S. government claimed the right to torture some people. What do you think about that?

I would like to thank Tanya Golash-Boza and James Tyner for their invaluable feedback. I would also like to thank France Winddance Twine for her encouragement.

1: Why Are We (Still) Talking about Torture?

Every single day I think and read about **torture**. Some days I write about it, or teach about it. I can turn any social conversation to the topic within minutes. (Keep that in mind if we meet for coffee.) I will be the first to admit that my interest in torture, which has been building over several decades, is unusually intense. In this book I share some of the insights that thinking about torture all this time has yielded.

Thinking about torture is a far less lonely preoccupation these days than it was before the turn of this century. The fact that more people are thinking and talking about torture is both heartening and alarming. It is heartening because torture is an important issue that deserves people's attention. It is alarming because what many more people are talking about these days is *American torture*. At the dawn of the 21st century the U.S. government was not invested in the business of torture. Sure, through-out the 20th century there were a number of places where the United States supported torturing regimes that were our allies or turned a blind eye when doing so was deemed by officials to be in the national interest (see Chapter 3). But the principle that torture was wrong and illegal was accepted by almost anyone who thought about it.

What changed? The answer arises from the devastating terrorist attacks of **September 11, 2001 (9/11)** that killed almost 3,000 people. The government responded by launching a global "**war on terror**." In the context of that **war**, authorization to use tactics widely regarded as torture on people suspected of being terrorists or enemy fighters came from the highest echelons of the government. Some American soldiers, Central Intelligence Agency (CIA) agents, and government-hired contractors did the deeds. Although the government has tried to get out of the torture business in recent years, that legacy is now part of our national history. It can never be erased.

By way of illustrating how many more people are thinking about torture these days, consider this: Between 1995 and 1999, there were 12 scenes of torture on primetime network television. In contrast, between 2002 and 2007, there were 897 (Human Rights First 2007). That massive jump indicates that TV writers, directors, and producers, whose jobs depend on being able to create shows that would appeal to viewers, believed that storylines involving torture were what the audience wanted. What many shows gave their viewers were plots literally "ripped from the headlines," to borrow the tag line of the long-running series *Law and Order*.

Since 2001, torture—American torture, that is—has been episodically headlining news and the topic of public debates. It is no surprise, then, that torture became an increasingly popular part of primetime entertainment, depicted not only in "old" ways as the work of evil people but in "new" ways as heroic and necessary. An example of this heroic view of torture was the top-rated Fox show *24*. The main character, Jack Bauer (played by Kiefer Sutherland), was an unsquemish vigilante who would torture people for information to "keep Americans safe."

The alarming part of this burgeoning interest in torture is that growing numbers of Americans have become increasingly open to the idea of torture, if not actively endorsing it (Gronke, et al. 2010). According to a 2008 public opinion poll, the use of torture under certain circumstances was acceptable to 44 percent of Americans, up from 36 percent in 2006 (Kull, et al. 2008). According to a poll published days before the ten-year anniversary of 9/11, a 53 percent *majority* said that torture is justified "often" or "sometimes" (Lobe 2011).

Take a moment to think about how you would answer the question of whether torture is ever justified. Then think about the fact that your views might change by the time you reach the end of this book. Whatever you think, at least you are thinking about torture. Welcome to my world!

Torture Gets a Makeover

In the wake of the 9/11 terrorist attacks, suddenly torture was being thought and talked about in a new way. On *Meet the Press* on September 16, 2001, Vice President Dick Cheney said:

> We'll have to work … the dark side, if you will. We've got to spend time in the shadows in the intelligence world. A lot of what needs to be done here will have to be done quietly, without any discussion, using sources and methods that are available to our intelligence agencies—if we are going to be successful … [I]t's going to be vital for us to use any means at our disposal … to achieve our objectives.

On September 26, Cofer Black, a counter-terrorism expert, testified in Congress that there "was a before 9/11 and an after 9/11, and after 9/11 the gloves came off." Black's "gloves off" euphemism, along with Cheney's using "any means at our disposal" signaled that decision makers were contemplating violent interrogation methods because they assumed these would be useful to elicit information necessary to win the war on terror and keep Americans safe. However, for the first few years, the policies that resulted were largely unknown to the public because they were, in Cheney's words, "done quietly, without any discussion."

Meanwhile, the American public demonstrated a parallel willingness to reconsider the torture taboo. Many people started debating whether we (Americans) should torture terrorists. The centerpiece of these public debates was the **hypothetical ticking bomb scenario**. In this scenario, a bomb is set to explode and the lives of hundreds, thousands, or even millions of people are at risk (depending on the nature and location of this hypothetical bomb). The person who knows where the bomb is and how to defuse it has been captured. However, he or she is refusing to divulge the information. Should torture be used to extract that information from the recalcitrant terrorist in order to avert a catastrophic attack and save innocent lives?

Some people argued that under certain exceptional circumstances, of which the ticking bomb scenario was a perfect example, torture might be necessary and, thus, legitimate. They could be called **pro-torture consequentialists**. Consequentialism is a class of ethical theory that holds that the morality of conduct should be judged on the basis of its outcome or consequences. If, they argued, torture produces the information to save those lives, then using torture under those circumstances cannot be wrong. On an October 27, 2001 segment of CNN's *Crossfire*, commentator Tucker Carlson said, "Torture is bad. [But] some things are worse. And under some circumstances, it may be the lesser of two evils." This quote exemplifies the pro-torture proposition that torture is a "lesser evil" than terrorism.

Alan Dershowitz, a Harvard University law professor, was a prolific advocate for exceptions to the prohibition (2002a, 2003, 2004). Citing the hypothetical ticking bomb scenario, he wrote:

> I have absolutely no doubt that [American law enforcement officers] would try to torture the terrorists into providing the information. Moreover, the vast majority of Americans would expect the officers to engage in that time-tested technique for loosening tongues, notwithstanding our unequivocal treaty obligations never to employ torture, no matter how exigent the circumstances. The real question is not whether torture would be used—it would—but whether it would be used outside of the law or within the law.
>
> (Dershowitz 2002b)

He suggested that the use of torture could be brought within the law by empowering special judges to issue "torture warrants."

In order to hold the line at lesser evil and not slide into the terrain of absolute evil, the pro-torture consequentialists insisted on limits to the kinds of techniques that would be permissible. The terrorist could not be boiled in oil or put on the rack. That would be uncivilized! Rather, he or she could be subjected to what these folks liked to refer to as "**torture lite**"—tactics that do not permanently damage or destroy the body. Dershowitz's suggestion was sterilized needles under the fingernails. "I wanted to come up with a tactic that can't possibly cause permanent physical

harm but is excruciatingly painful ... I want maximal pain, minimum lethality"
(Hansen 2002).

On the other side of post-9/11 debates about torture and the moral philosophy of
national security were those who argued that no cause or crisis justifies the erosion of
the absolute prohibition against torture and, therefore, using torture would be immoral
as well as illegal. They could be called **anti-torture deontologists**. Deontology (from
the Greek *deon*, meaning "obligation, duty") is a class of ethical theory that holds that
the morality of conduct should be judged on the basis of rules, not on good intentions
or outcomes. Variations on this theme included arguments that there is no such thing
as just a little torture; once you start torturing terrorists you open the door to torturing
anyone in the future, and using torture makes you no better than your enemy (see
Greenberg 2005).

The pro-torture consequentialists were inclined to reference the past death and
destruction of 9/11 to rationalize the necessity of future torture, and they tried to
shame those who oppose torture under all circumstances by arguing that the latter
were less concerned about the safety of innocent victims than the sanctity of legal
principles and/or the **rights** of terrorists. But their arguments depended entirely on
the belief that torture *works*. Certainly some people can be "broken" under torture to
divulge information, but the hypothetical ticking bomb scenario that is so popular
and important to pro-torture arguments is highly (if not entirely) implausible in any
real-world setting. Kim Scheppele (2005) persuasively debunks the scenario using a
sociological approach to inquire "into whether distinctions drawn in abstract moral or
legal debate track the actual contexts of decisions when hard choices have to be made
'on the ground'" (p. 291). She highlights the following problems:

> First, the hypothetical assumes that you (as the moral agent to whom the hypo-
> thetical is directed) and the terrorist are alone in the world ... There is no insti-
> tutional context ... But of course in any real-world context, the choice would
> be made in an institutional setting by those charged with the responsibility to
> fight terrorism. The question, therefore, is not whether "you" as an individual
> should torture, but instead whether a nation should have a policy approving the
> use of torture—a very different moral matter ... Second, the hypothetical
> assumes an extraordinary degree of clarity about the situation [the existence of
> a bomb set to explode] in which you (now an institutional "you") find yourself
> when the question of whether to torture arises ... Such certainty may be hypo-
> thetically possible, but it will likely never exist. Instead, it is far more likely that
> you will wonder whether there is a bomb in the first place and, if there is, how
> dangerous it might be. Third, the hypothetical assumes that the person to be
> tortured is the one (perhaps even the only one) who knows where the ticking
> bomb is ... [I]t is highly unlikely that any person faced with the decision to
> torture will know whether the suspect ... has the relevant information ... Instead,

the more likely question will be whether the person to be tortured really knows anything useful at all. Finally, the hypothetical assumes that if the captured person gives you the information after being tortured, the information will in fact be true and useful in defusing the bomb. Yet torture produces results that are highly unreliable.

(pp. 292–93)

Scheppele's article injected a dose of reality into public debates to counter popular but implausible propositions. The problems she identifies, especially the unreliability of information elicited through torture, are supported by abundant evidence and expert opinion that violent and degrading interrogation tactics are actually ineffective as a practical matter and devastating as a policy choice. I return to these issues in Chapter 6.

The Slow Drip of Public Information

Although hypothetical arguments did not subside, public discourse about torture started broadening as information about the treatment of *actual* prisoners in U.S. custody began to emerge. A starting point for this shift occurred on November 13, 2001, when President George W. Bush issued a military order decreeing that captured terror suspects were "**unlawful combatants**." Under the laws of war, everyone involved in or affected by armed conflict falls into one of two categories: combatants (i.e. soldiers) who have a right to fight, and civilians who don't have a right to fight (except under exceptional circumstances of self-defense) but who do have the right not to be targeted or otherwise treated as combatants. The Bush administration conceived of "unlawful combatants" to deny that people captured in the war on terror have any rights, including the right to **habeas corpus**, a customary law obligation requiring the government to show cause for why a person is being imprisoned. With this new order, the president asserted that he had the unilateral authority to classify anyone as an unlawful combatant without any obligation to show cause. What this meant in practice was that anyone taken into custody and classified as an unlawful combatant was presumed guilty and could be indefinitely detained.

On January 11, 2002, the first unlawful combatants captured abroad were transported to the U.S. naval base at **Guantánamo** Bay on the south side of the island of Cuba. They were denounced by officials in the press as "the worst of the worst." The presumption was that *these* were the people who had caused 9/11. The Pentagon released photos of these prisoners in **stress positions** (i.e. bound and immobilized in physically straining positions) and **sensory deprivation** gear (i.e. padded mittens, ear muffs, and goggles). They were housed in open-air cages in a part of the base called Camp X-Ray (see Greenberg 2009).

Figure 1.1 The first prisoners detained at Guantánamo.
Source: U.S. Navy.

Guantánamo had been selected as the main site to interrogate and detain unlawful combatants because it was far from the hot war zone of Afghanistan and, more importantly, because Bush administration officials believed prisoners held there would be beyond the reach of U.S. courts. Aside from the photos, nothing about the Guantánamo prisoners was made public, including their identities or how they were being treated by interrogators and guards. The prison was branded a "legal black hole" by some critics.

On December 26, 2002, *The Washington Post* published a groundbreaking investigative article by Dana Priest and Barton Gellman, which revealed that, in the drive for **actionable intelligence** (information of security value), U.S. agents were utilizing "stress and duress tactics" to interrogate people captured in Afghanistan and elsewhere, and detainees who could not be broken by such methods might be given mind-altering drugs or subject to "**extraordinary rendition**" (i.e. kidnapped and secretly transported for questioning) to foreign governments with well-established records of torture, such as Egypt and Morocco. According to Priest and Gellman, "While the US government publicly denounces the use of torture, each of the current national security officials interviewed for this article defended the use of violence against captives as just and necessary. They expressed confidence that the American public would back their view."

Over the following year, more information became public as a result of journalistic exposés (e.g. Bowden 2003; Rose 2004a) and reports by **human rights** monitors (Amnesty International 2002; Human Rights Watch 2003). What people increasingly were talking about was reflected in the title of John Parry's (2003) article, "What Is Torture, Are We Doing It, and What If We Are?"

It's Not Hypothetical!

The "it's not hypothetical!" phase began abruptly on April 28, 2004, when CBS's *60 Minutes II* broadcast photos of naked, abused, humiliated, bloodied, and dead prisoners from the **Abu Ghraib** prison in Iraq. The context was provided by the simultaneously published online version of Seymour Hersh's (2004) *New Yorker* article on the leaked ("not meant for public release") *Taguba Report* (2004). When word of prisoner abuse at Abu Ghraib had reached the Pentagon the previous December, Major General Antonio Taguba was tasked to lead an investigation. His report concluded that the abuses at Abu Ghraib were "systematic" and "wanton." Those photos and the *Taguba Report* completely changed the conversation about torture.

The Bush administration's initial response to the Abu Ghraib scandal was to blame a few "bad apples." Brigadier General Mark Kimmitt said, "All of us are disappointed by the actions of the few … but by God, it doesn't reflect my army." Defense Secretary Donald Rumsfeld, during a surprise visit to Iraq on May 14, told troops at Abu Ghraib, "In recent days there's been a focus on a few that have betrayed our values and sullied the reputation of our country," adding that their actions do not represent "the values of America."

The Abu Ghraib photos, which had gone instantly viral, made the scandal a global phenomenon (Walsh 2003). Officials appeared before Congressional committees to

Figure 1.2 Prisoner abuse at Abu Ghraib in Iraq.
Source: The Abu Ghraib Files.

testify about how Abu Ghraib had happened. The "bad apple" excuse was not satisfactory to questioners who wanted to know more about the government's secret prisoner policies. As a result, in June 2004 the Bush administration declassified the first batch of legal memos and policy documents pertaining to military and CIA interrogations. These documents were nicknamed "**torture memos**" because they exposed how officials had sanctioned violent and degrading interrogation tactics, and how the laws had been reinterpreted to evade the consequences for engaging in punishable crimes.

How the United States Became a Torturing Regime

The torture memos revealed that the clandestine drive to unfetter the executive branch from the laws that prohibit torture and inhumane treatment started in January 2002. White House Counsel Alberto Gonzales (who later became attorney general) asked the Defense Department to instruct intelligence officers at Guantánamo to fill out a one-page form on each detainee certifying the president's "reason to believe" that that person was involved in terrorism. Within weeks, the officers began reporting back that interrogations were not producing the information needed to fulfill this request. Officials presumed that legal restraints on interrogation were the problem, and that harsher methods were necessary to get those terrorists to talk (Mayer 2008; Rose 2004b).

But because of the importance of law and legality in American culture and society, the U.S. government could not do what brutal dictatorships do—just ignore the laws prohibiting torture. Rather, officials had to figure out a way to make what they wanted to do appear "legal." The main obstacle was the **Geneva Conventions 1949**, the centerpiece of **international humanitarian law (IHL)** (which forms part of the laws of war). These conventions are "law of the land" in the United States, and are enshrined in the Uniform Code of Military Justice, which regulates all four branches of the armed forces. The Geneva Conventions expressly prohibit torture and cruel treatment of *any* prisoners captured in war. The United Nations **Convention against Torture and Other Cruel, Inhuman, or Degrading Treatment or Punishment (CAT)**, a **human rights law**, is also law of the land. After the United States ratified the CAT treaty in 1994, Congress passed a federal law to make it enforceable in U.S. courts. I elaborate on these laws in Chapter 4.

The first obstacle was cleared on February 7, 2002, when President Bush, acting on the advice of lawyers in the White House and Justice Department's **Office of Legal Counsel (OLC)**, issued a secret directive to his national security team declaring that the Geneva Conventions do not apply to the war on terror. He ignored the advice of the State Department that had sharply criticized the legal flaws and political dangers of this position. As the torture memos revealed, government lawyers advised that if the president, in his capacity as commander-in-chief, *declared* that the laws of war do not apply, there can be no war crime! Lawyers also advised that federal laws are not enforceable outside the territorial jurisdiction of the United States. Therefore, any violations perpetrated at Guantánamo or elsewhere overseas were not punishable crimes in U.S. courts if those who engaged in the violations were acting on the president's orders and in the interests of national security (see Greenberg and Dratel 2005; Horton 2007; Jaffer and Singh 2007).

In the division of interrogational labor, the CIA was vested with primary responsibility for **"high-value detainees" (HVDs)**—people assumed to be terrorist leaders or to have knowledge about terrorist operations and plots. On March 28, 2002, the first HVD, Abu Zubaydah (*nom du guerre* for Zayn al-Abidin Muhammad), was captured in Pakistan and transported to a **black site** (the term for secret prisons run by the CIA) in Thailand. The escalating harshness of Abu Zubaydah's treatment, including **waterboarding** him 83 times and placing him in a coffin-like confinement box, was due to CIA interrogators' frustration that he was not providing the actionable intelligence he was assumed to possess. (Years later, the government would acknowledge that, contrary to initial claims, he was not actually a "top al-Qaeda strategist.")

By the summer of 2002, some CIA agents were growing anxious about their vulnerability to future prosecution for what they had been authorized to do to Abu Zubaydah. In response to the agency's questions about legal liability for torture, the OLC produced two memos dated August 1, 2002. The first memo interpreted the applicable definition of *physical torture* to exclude anything less severe than "the pain accompanying serious physical injury, such as organ failure, impairment of bodily function, or even death," and opined that cruel, inhuman, or degrading treatment would not constitute *mental torture* unless it caused effects that lasted "months or even years." The second memo provided legal cover for tactics already in use.

Although these OLC memos were written for the CIA, which is a civilian agency, the White House forwarded them to the Pentagon, which was seeking a solution to military interrogators' frustrated efforts to get actionable intelligence out of Guantánamo detainees. A three-course menu of tactics authorized by Defense Secretary Rumsfeld in December 2002 included the use of military dogs, protracted sleep deprivation and stress positions, forced nudity, and beatings. When top military lawyers in the Judge Advocate General (JAG) corps reviewed this policy document, they wrote memos to Rumsfeld protesting that the use of such tactics would expose soldiers to the risk of court martial. Their dissent and warnings were ignored.

Talking about Torture after Abu Ghraib

The torture memos cast a different light on the abuses depicted in the Abu Ghraib photos and provided material evidence that military interrogators, CIA agents, and government contractors had been, in effect, licensed by the Bush administration to utilize methods that were no longer regulated by the laws of this nation or the world. But the Bush administration never acknowledged the authorization of "torture."

Rather, officials claimed that tactics authorized by the administration were "not torture" because they had been deemed "legal" by OLC lawyers.

In order to dodge the torture label, officially authorized methods were euphemized as "**enhanced interrogation techniques**." They included stripping prisoners naked, short-shackling them to the floor for protracted periods of time, forcing them to defecate and urinate on themselves; subjecting prisoners to days or weeks of sleep deprivation by bombarding them with constant light and/or excruciatingly loud music or grating sounds and/or extremes in temperature; weeks, months, or even years of isolation; stress positions such as "long time standing," which entails forcing prisoners to stand still for many hours, sometimes with arms extended outward, and "wall hanging" from hooks on the wall or ceiling; "walling," which referred to bashing prisoners into walls; and waterboarding to induce the feeling and fear of death by drowning. Waterboarding was the hardest to pass off as "not torture" because it was a classic method used by medieval Inquisitors and Nazis, and because in the 20th century people were prosecuted in U.S. courts for using it (Nance 2007).

What kinds of responses did these revelations generate? Some pro-torture advocates, echoing official statements, insisted that these tactics are necessary, effective, and "not torture." However, the Bush administration faced some Congressional push-back from three so-called "Republican dissenters" in the Senate. John McCain, a torture survivor from the Vietnam War, Lindsey Graham, a reservist JAG officer, and John Warner, chair of the Armed Services Committee, were angry that the administration's authorization of coercive and degrading techniques exposed soldiers to the risk of court martial and this threatened to undermine military discipline. In October 2005, Congress passed the McCain amendment that (re)prohibited inhumane and degrading treatment by military interrogators. But a majority of legislators, including McCain, conceded to Cheney's demand for a "CIA exception" allowing agents and contractors to continue using tactics that the military was no longer permitted to use.

What about the general public? There were some small-scale demonstrations and online petition drives protesting torture. But the majority of Americans were, at best, indifferent to revelations about the abusive, violent, and degrading treatment of prisoners. Public indifference may be explained in part by the fact that the people subjected to these no-longer-secret tactics were foreign Muslims captured in war. No domestic constituency perceived itself as imperiled by the government's authorization of such practices. Another explanation is the fact that the legal arguments and issues implicated in wartime interrogation policies were very complicated.

Challenging Torture in Court

Because the Bush administration had essentially "legalized" torture, some lawyers and legal intellectuals emerged as the most dedicated and visible critics. Contrary to right-wing partisan contentions, opposition to interrogational abuse was not monopolized by leftists and liberals. Hundreds of American lawyers—Republicans as well as Democrats, military lawyers as well as civilians—devoted themselves to challenging the authorization and use of torture and inhumane treatment by taking cases to court. Thus, courts became a battlefield in the war on terror.

The Bush administration denounced such litigation and sought—usually successfully—to persuade judges that claims relating to the treatment of unlawful combatants are not their business. The **state secrets privilege**, a doctrine which allows the government to withhold sensitive pieces of information if it is in the country's national security interest to do so, was used like a blanket to smother cases pertaining to the treatment of prisoners. The Bush administration's hostility to legal challenges was epitomized in the 2005 National Security Strategy of the United States, which includes the following line: "Our strength as a nation-state will continue to be challenged by those who employ a strategy of the weak using international fora [forums], judicial processes and terrorism."

A few cases did, however, make it all the way to the **Supreme Court**. In the *Rasul* v. *Bush* decision of 2004, the Court ruled that Guantánamo detainees cannot be denied habeas corpus rights indefinitely. Congress tried to gut that ruling by passing the Detainee Treatment Act (DTA) in 2005, which included a jurisdiction-stripping measure to block detainees' access to federal courts for habeas or torture claims. In the *Hamdan* v. *Rumsfeld* decision in June 2006, the Court ruled that the **military commissions** (special tribunals to prosecute Guantánamo detainees) were unconstitutional because they were created by presidential decree. The *Hamdan* decision also recognized that unlawful combatants have, at minimum, the rights and protections of **Common Article 3** of the Geneva Conventions, which prohibits "violence to life and person, in particular murder of all kinds, mutilation, cruel treatment and torture" and "outrages upon personal dignity, in particular humiliating and degrading treatment."

At a September 6, 2006 press conference, President Bush denounced the *Hamdan* decision and mocked the vagueness of "outrages." He also acknowledged for the first time the existence of the CIA's interrogation and detention program and that he personally had approved waterboarding and other "alternative techniques." He announced that 14 HVDs in CIA custody, including the self-proclaimed "mastermind" of 9/11, Khalid Sheikh Muhammad (KSM), were being transferred to Guantánamo. In October, Congress passed the **Military Commissions Act (MCA)** to resurrect the tribunal system that the Supreme Court had cancelled. The MCA included even bolder jurisdiction-stripping language than the DTA, as well as a clause to grant *ex post facto* immunity for violations of the War Crimes Act to shield government officials and state agents from future prosecution for violations of Common Article 3. (The MCA was revised in 2009, but the immunity clause remains.)

The Bush administration continued to defend its interrogation policies, despite the growing amount of information available to the public that torture was not effective and that it damaged U.S. national interests. This was the conclusion of a 2008 report by the bipartisan U.S. Senate Armed Services Committee that determined that the use of aggressive techniques and the redefining of law to create the appearance of their legality "damaged our ability to collect accurate intelligence that could save lives, strengthened the hand of our enemies, and compromised our moral authority." There also was abundant evidence that many of the people who had been caught up in the war on terror and imprisoned for years were innocent. Of the 779 people ever detained at Guantánamo, more than 550 were released or transferred by the time Bush left office.

The Legacy of American Torture

During the 2008 campaign season, the torture debacle barely registered as an election issue; the nation was consumed by the economic meltdown. But to their credit, both presidential candidates—Republican McCain and Democrat Barack Obama—vaunted their anti-torture credentials on occasion. While Obama promised to end torture and restore the rule of law, to demonstrate his aspirations to reunite a divided nation, he skirted questions about criminal accountability for officials who were responsible for torture with the rhetoric of wanting to "look forward, not backward."

On his second day in office, President Obama signed an executive order requiring CIA interrogators to adhere to the same rules that apply to the military, and he shuttered the black sites. But initiatives to close Guantánamo, which Obama had vowed to do within one year, became fodder for attacks that his administration was pandering to the "far left" and was "soft on terror." Congress passed laws to make it virtually impossible to close Guantánamo and required the use of military commissions rather than federal courts to prosecute terror suspects.

Cheney, renowned for his secretive silence, became uncharacteristically talkative after he was out of office. He defended the Bush administration's record by propounding the message that brutal interrogation tactics (which he described as "tough" but not "torture") had produced "excellent intelligence" that had kept the nation safe, as "proven" by the fact that there were no "massive-casualty attacks" in the United States after 9/11, and he criticized the Obama administration for relinquishing methods that "work." Cheney's media offensive emboldened the pro-torture consequentialists to dominate public debates about interrogation policy past, present, and future.

Nevertheless, there were people who spoke out against American torture. In 2008 testimony before Congress, Alberto Mora, one of the top JAGs who criticized Rumsfeld's authorization of abusive tactics back in 2002–03, said:

> To use so-called "harsh" interrogation techniques during the war on terror was a mistake of massive proportions. It damaged and continues to damage our nation. This policy, which may be aptly called a "policy of cruelty," violated our

founding values, our constitutional system and the fabric of our laws, our over-arching foreign policy interests and our national security. The net effect of this policy of cruelty has been to weaken our defenses, not to strengthen them.

Taguba, who authored the investigative report on Abu Ghraib, said:

> After years of disclosures by government investigations, media accounts, and reports from human rights organizations, there is no longer any doubt as to whether the [Bush] administration has committed war crimes. The only question that remains to be answered is whether those who ordered the use of torture will be held to account.
>
> (Taguba 2008)

To date, there has been no real accountability for officials who authorized the use of torture. Some people think the Obama administration's cancelation of waterboarding and other violent and degrading tactics was a mistake, and would endorse their resurrection. Thus, as a nation we have not come to terms with the legacy. That is the reason we are *still* talking about torture.

DISCUSSION QUESTIONS

1. If you were drawn into a debate about torture right now, would you argue that it is sometimes "necessary" and therefore "legitimate"? Why or why not?
2. The Bush administration authorized the use of waterboarding and other "enhanced interrogation techniques" on terror suspects. When these methods were exposed to the public, officials claimed that these are "not torture." What was the basis of their reasoning?
3. If you were to exercise your civic rights and write a letter to your political representative in Congress about one issue raised in this chapter, which issue would you focus on and what point would you want to convey?

II: Torture's Past

In this chapter, I present a history of torture and its legal abolition, focusing mainly on Europe. Torture played a central role in the evolution of law–state–society relations from ancient times to the early modern era. The questions explored here are: What purposes did torture serve? Who was subjected to torture and why? Why did torture eventually come to be seen as a problem rather than a solution to maintaining law and order?

The Invention of Torture

The ancient Greeks invented **judicial torture**, which refers to painful questioning to extract information for a *legal process*. **Penal torture**, which refers to painful forms of *punishment*, has a much longer history—it is as old as human society (Garland 1990: 18).

There are differences of opinion among historians about where to draw the line between torture and not torture in the ancient and pre-modern eras. This distinction is not based on the intensity or the amount of torment. Rather, it turns on whether to regard painful punishments as torture. John Langbein is emphatic: "No punishment, no matter how gruesome, should be called torture" (2006: 3). Edward Peters agrees that "judicial torture is the *only* kind of torture" (1996: 7).

Michel Foucault's (1977) *Discipline and Punish* is not a history of torture per se, but it is one of the most influential books in sociology (Simon 1998), among other fields, and, thus, one of the most widely read accounts of torture's past. Foucault has no qualms about combining judicial and penal torture, which he characterizes as the "gloomy festival of punishment" (p. 8), because he is interested in how and why rulers exercised their power to attack the bodies of their subjects.

To introduce the historic purposes that torture served in law–state–society complexes where the use of physical violence was deemed necessary and legal, think of it this way: Judicial and penal torture were, respectively, the painful *means* and *ends* of law enforcement processes.

Antiquity

Judicial torture began when Greek society transitioned from a communal system to a more complex system with the rise of the *polis* (city-state). Justice was transformed from private *feuds* between individuals and households into public laws and the resolution of conflicts through *trials*. Torture was instituted to provide *legal evidence* for trials. The etymology (word history) of torture traces back to *basanos*, Greek for a touchstone used to test gold for purity. According to Paige DuBois (1991: 14), "The 'test,' over time, changes to 'torture,' as the analogy is extended to the testing of human bodies in juridical procedures for the Athenian courts."

It was the Greek *slave* and under certain circumstances the foreigner, but never the *citizen*, who could be "tested" through torture. The rationales for slave torture were premised on ideas that (*a*) a slave's servile status made it impossible for him or her to make spontaneously truthful statements because (*b*) fear of being punished by the owner would incline the slave to lie, and therefore (*c*) only through pain would slaves speak truth. Tortured statements from slaves were evidence, not **confessions** (admissions of one's own criminal behavior); slaves didn't have the "right" to be put on trial and their punishments were not regulated by courts.

But if torture was perceived as an effective means to produce truth, why limit it to slaves? In the larger context of ancient Greece society, torture helped mark an absolute difference in status between slaves, who lacked "honor," and even the lowliest freemen. According to Greek social ideology, truth was assumed to be *embodied* in slaves and extractable only by torturing their bodies, whereas freemen produced truth through *reasoned speech*. Because freemen were equally capable of lying as of speaking the truth, the value of tortured slave speech was, paradoxically, elevated by the value of freemen's reason and honor.

The ancient Romans were influenced by the Greeks. In earliest **Roman law**, only slaves could be tortured. But as Roman government and society got more complex and developed into an empire, social divisions were reconfigured into status categories of *honestiores* (the privileged governing class) and *humiliores* (everyone else). *Humiliores* could be subjected to judicial torture, and those found guilty could face painful punishments and humiliating executions that earlier had been reserved for slaves.

The relationship between Roman law and torture evolved as a result of the expanding spectrum of crimes and changes in criminal procedure. Judicial interrogation (*quaestio*) and tormenting punishment (*tormentum*) were joined together into questioning by torment (*quaestio per tormenta*). The use of torture by the Roman state had the slippery slope effect of eroding the privilege of not being subject to torture. Eventually even *honestiores* could be tortured as defendants or witnesses in cases of treason and, over time, for "a broader and broader spectrum of cases determined by imperial order" (Peters 1996: 18).

The term "excruciating" traces back to the Latin *cruciare*, meaning to crucify or torture. The crucifixion of Jesus of Nazareth in the Roman province of Judea was an example of the kind of brutal punishment used on slaves, rebels, and despised categories of criminals. The crucified were displayed naked in public; were vulnerable to attacks by crowds, wild beasts, and birds of prey; were subject to prolonged suffering; and when dead they were denied a proper burial.

By the last quarter of the 1st century AD/CE, Christians (monotheistic followers of Jesus) were regarded by Roman rulers as impious and subversive, and Christianity was regarded as a form of treason. Christians were tortured both to confirm their lowly and despised status and to deter the evangelical spread of their beliefs. However, after Christianity was adopted as the religion of the Roman imperial state in the 4th century, heresy (beliefs that deviate from religious orthodoxy) and acts committed against churches or clergy were made into public offenses. Thus, the use of torture to defend Christianity was "legal" by the time the **Roman Empire** collapsed.

Between the 5th and 6th centuries (late antiquity), Germanic invaders (barbarians) took over the regions of Western Europe once ruled by the Roman Empire. Social order and justice were maintained through custom-based laws. Accusations of wrongdoing were resolved by making parties to a conflict swear oaths, or engage in duels or judicial combat where the winner was declared the person in the right. Under **trials by ordeal**—for example, making a person accused of wrongdoing walk on burning coals or stick a hand in boiling water to retrieve a stone—it was believed that an omniscient and just God would intervene, perhaps by miracle, to save the innocent. Although ordeals involved pain and suffering, the role of God distinguished them from judicial torture.

Medieval Europe

Judicial torture experienced a revival in Europe starting in the 12th century due to a combination of factors. One was the rediscovery of Roman law that provided an appealing model as political power was becoming more concentrated and societies and economies more developed in medieval Europe. Another factor was the culturally declining confidence in God's arbitrating abilities and the desire for *human* competence to decide innocence and guilt. In 1215, the Church of Rome forbade clergy from participating in ordeals. A third factor was the shift from a justice model based on accusations to one based on inquisitions—inquiring about truth through professional means to gather evidence and witness testimony, to interrogate suspects for confessions, and to try the accused on the basis of such evidence.

Under inquisitorial procedures, confessions became "the queen of proofs." The importance of confessions was elevated by the fact that *circumstantial evidence* was not admissible for serious crimes. Without either two unimpeachable *eyewitnesses* or a confession, there could be no conviction. For example, if a man was found holding a bloody knife next to a dead body but no one had seen him stab the other person, the bloody knife was circumstantial evidence and he could not be convicted of murder unless he confessed. Consequently, torturing people to get them to confess to crimes became a key tool of law and order. Most medieval European states relied on torture to investigate serious crimes within their jurisdiction.

In 1252, Pope Innocent IV authorized Holy Inquisitors to use torture in their investigations of heresy. In the early medieval period, *belief* in witchery (allegations that people were communing or conspiring with Satan) was regarded as a form of heresy. That changed in 1326 when Pope John XXII authorized inquisitors to treat witchery as a form of heresy. Confessions—and, thus, torture—were especially important for investigating and prosecuting categories of crimes involving one's beliefs, like heresy, or clandestine behavior unlikely to be witnessed by innocent others, like sodomy or witchery. Torture was used to probe people about their guilt or to break those who proclaimed their innocence, to force them to provide details about their crimes, and, perhaps, to name co-conspirators.

The Black Death, a pandemic that peaked in Europe between 1348 and 1350 and killed between 30 and 60 percent of the continent's population, nourished suspicions and fears of evil forces. This led to centuries of inquisitions, religious strife, and social unrest. The Protestant Reformation initiated in 1517 when Martin Luther posted his 95 theses protesting the doctrines, rituals, and corruption of the Catholic Church, and the Church's Counter-Reformation intensified religious wars and political conflicts across the continent, culminating in the Thirty Years' War (1618–48). Many historians attribute the dramatic rise in witch hunting to these destabilizing and devastating events. People accused or suspected of being witches, the vast majority of whom were women, were subjected to judicial torture and were punished in ways that usually ended in death, burning being the most common.

Torturing people for confessions was a routine, judicially supervised procedure. A confession elicited through torture had to be repeated after the torture ended, but if the person retracted the statement, the torture could resume. Many laws regulated how and on whom torture should be used. Foucault accurately described medieval torture as "cruel but not savage" and as the "art of maintaining life in pain" (1977: 40, 33–34) because it was done by professional torturers who used various and specified techniques and instruments.

In Foucault's analysis of the "gloomy festival of punishments," he identifies four characteristics of medieval torture: (*a*) It must produce *legally prescribed degrees of pain* (i.e. neither more nor less than the law allows); (*b*) the pain must *correspond to the crime* (e.g. piercing the tongues of blasphemers, assaulting the genitals of adulterers); (*c*) the tortured body must be *ritually marked* to function as a symbol of the crime and a warning to others; and (*d*) punishment must be *spectacular and public* to deter crime and to foster a public consciousness about social order and the power of the law.

Although torture was legal and routine, its "basic flaw" was no secret. What it proved was the individual's capacity to endure pain rather than the truth of any statements elicited. As Langbein (1978: 8) states, "Judicial torture survived the centuries not because its defects had been concealed, but in spite of their having been

Figure 2.1 The Marquise de Brinvilliers being tortured with water before her beheading.
Source: F. Monchablon.

long revealed." The **paradox of pre-modern torture** was that it was both necessary to enforce the law and a dubious means of eliciting truth.

Unlike continental Europe, England did not adopt Roman law. Rather, English law developed from a more archaic decentralized model (similar to late antiquity), with "legal institutions so crude that torture was unnecessary" (Langbein 2006: 77). By the 13th century, English common law had acquired most of its fundamental characteristics, including the admissibility of circumstantial evidence and the jury trial ("the rough justice of the countryside"). Thus, English law enforcement did not need confessions the way continental law did.

However, the English state instituted torture during the Tudor–Stuart period. After King Henry VIII broke with the Church of Rome (to marry Anne Boleyn) and established the Church of England, the country entered a protracted period of religious wars and political unrest. English rulers, fearing that Catholic subjects were colluding with Spain, authorized torture warrants to investigate treasonous plots and to root out heresy (including dissent from the Church of England). But, as William Blackstone explained, the rack "was an engine of the state, not of law." The experiment with torture ended before the English Bill of Rights was passed in 1689.

Making Torture Taboo

In the late 18th century, European legal systems were reformed to eliminate judicial torture, and by 1800 almost no traces were left. The **abolition of torture** coincided with moves to disallow some punishments that involved public humiliation, protracted physical suffering, and bodily disfigurement (e.g. racking, drawing and quartering, burning at the stake, and mutilation). The guillotine was invented to be an efficient and painless form of execution.

Although **Enlightenment thought** and a new spirit of **humanitarianism** were factors in the abolition of torture (Hunt 2007), many scholars contend that a variety of changes in law–state–society complexes must be taken into account. Langbein (1978, 2006) emphasizes the importance of changes in criminal procedure, including reforms allowing people to be convicted for serious crimes on the basis of circumstantial evidence. Others emphasize the development of modern forms of imprisonment as alternatives to execution or excruciating pain (Foucault 1977).

The **de-legitimization of torture** is related to its legal abolition but derives more squarely from changing models of sovereign statehood (see Chapter 3). The American and French revolutions to establish democratic forms of government reconfigured relations between states and people, and the legal rights of each. The key architects of these revolutionary transformations advanced ideas that "all men" had "inalienable rights" and "dignity," and that government powers should be limited by law. Torture was regarded as incompatible with democracy because it represented "tyranny in microcosm" (Luban 2005:1,438).

In America, the de-legitimization of torture traces back to the founding of the republic. The **Eighth Amendment to the US Constitution**, passed in 1791, prohibits "cruel and unusual punishments." Along with habeas corpus (the Great Writ that prohibits officials from imprisoning someone without a good and legal reason) and the separation of powers to provide checks and balances on the branches of government, the ban on unconstitutional cruel treatment served as a foundation of the modern rule of law because it was understood as essential for conditions of liberty, limited government, and due process to thrive. Also, judicial torture to interrogate suspects contradicted one of the nation's founding legal principles: the *presumption of innocence*. However, court-ordered punishments of people found guilty, no matter how cruel the methods might seem, were lawful. Thus, the line-drawing between judicial and penal torture was complete: judicial torture was prohibited, and penal torture was folded into the law.

Colin Dayan (2007: 88) writes that the founding fathers selected the words "cruel and unusual" in the context of the decision to make slavery constitutional. In cases involving violence against slaves, judges often accepted that the *condition of slavery* necessitated certain cruelties, and only extreme and malicious abuse—for example, depriving slaves of food or clothing—would rise to the level of a constitutional violation.

After slavery was abolished at the end of the American Civil War, Dayan argues, legally permissible cruelties were transposed into the criminal justice system. Prisoners, like slaves, are "unfree." In contemporary cases pertaining to the treatment of prisoners, judges have accepted that the *conditions of imprisonment* may necessitate cruelties and deprivations, but these would not be unconstitutional violations unless they involve malicious intent or failure to provide for "identifiable human need such as food, warmth, or exercise." Thus, Dayan writes, the legacy of the slave era "still haunts our legal language and holds the prison system in thrall" (p. 16).

Echoes of this history of interpreting the law in such a way that certain classes of people have been deemed to have no right *not* to be subjected to violent and dehumanizing treatment can be heard in the legal reasoning in the "torture memos" (discussed in Chapter 1).

DISCUSSION QUESTIONS

1. In the historical account provided in this chapter, people were subjected to painful and violent treatment in the context of law enforcement for various purposes. Discuss and compare the purposes of "judicial torture," "penal torture," and "trials by ordeal."

2. Torture was a necessary and legitimate feature of law enforcement in some ancient societies and in medieval Europe, and then it was abolished. What are some of the reasons that explain this change?

3. "Cruel and unusual punishments" are unconstitutional in the United States, yet in the nation's legal system the death penalty and solitary confinement for long periods of time are not regarded (at least by courts) as per se violations of the Eighth Amendment. Discuss this issue.

III: Modern Torture

Torture, as you read in the previous chapter, was abolished as a legal procedure by 1800. In the 20th century, torture became a pervasive phenomenon around the globe (Forrest 1996). Why? In this chapter, I explain the rise of modern torture. Central to this explanation is the nature and the role of modern states and the politics of national security.

State Sovereignty and National (In)Security

The concept of **sovereignty** typically describes the power and authority of states. In the international system, sovereign states are equals (at least in principle). Think of the General Assembly of the United Nations, where each member-country has one vote. Sovereignty also is a way of framing and claiming **states' rights**, foremost the *right to independence* (political autonomy), the *right to rule over a specific territory and population* (domestic jurisdiction), and the *right to be free from outside intervention by other states* (non-interference).

In the pre-modern era, sovereign power was vested in the person of the king or queen. In the modern era, sovereignty is exercised through bureaucracies. The personalized rule and divine rights of kings have been replaced by *the politics of representative rule*. Modern states take many forms and some countries still have kings or queens. But all modern states base their sovereign right to rule (domestic authority and international recognition) on their status as the *institutional/bureaucratic* representative of their citizens. "The people" represented by the state usually are conceived as a nation, hence the concept of **nation-state**s. Even the most autocratic dictators *claim* that they rule on behalf of some sociopolitical constituency.

Modern states have duties as well as rights. The concept of **national security** combines the two principles: the state's duty and right to defend *society* and *itself* from threats. When officials perceive that their own power to rule is at risk, or when national interests are threatened, even the weakest states have the capacity to employ terrifying and deadly defenses. As Edward Peters (1996: 6–7) writes: "Paradoxically, in an age of vast state strength,... much of state policy has been based upon the concept of extreme state vulnerability to enemies, external or internal."

National security and the perceived insecurity of modern states is the main reason that torture made a comeback. The politics and practices of national security distinguish between "legitimate communities" and "enemies." The former are conceived as those members of the nation *in good standing* whose safety and security are the responsibility of the state to protect, and the latter are those categories of people deemed to threaten security who either "need" to be tortured (or executed, massacred, relocated, and so on) or who do not deserve not to be. In this regard, torturing people for national security reasons compares to warfare because both are forms of political violence directed at enemy "others" (see Ron 2003; Scarry 1985).

But the reasons *why* modern militaries, intelligence agencies, and police forces use torture vary. Understanding these variations involves a comparative consideration of the nature of the state and the particular (context-specific) interests and risks that drive official policies.

Why Modern States Torture

Judicial torture was revived or remained a feature in some legal systems that lack judicial impartiality and where confessions are the preferred or essential ingredient for convictions. In such systems, false tortured confessions may be as valuable as true ones if the state's objective is to persuade domestic constituencies that those being prosecuted and imprisoned or executed are guilty. Unlike judicial torture in the pre-modern era, modern states that use torture to get confessions do not publicly admit that they do so because torture is illegal and illegitimate.

In some countries, especially those in which post-revolutionary regimes strived to purge ideological and political enemies, tortured confessions were the prelude to stage show trials where "enemies of the state" were trotted out to renounce their own errors in opposing the regime. Ervand Abrahamian (1999), who studied tortured confessions in the Islamic Republic of Iran, describes how such confessions—presented as "recantations" of deviant thought and action—were broadcast as "interviews" on Iranian television and widely viewed. He writes: "These tapes bear striking and eerie resemblance to recantations produced elsewhere—especially in Maoist China during the 1945–54 'brainwashing' campaign and the 1965–71 Cultural Revolution; [and] in Stalinist Russia and Eastern Europe, first during the 1935–39 Moscow Trials and later in 1951–54 during the so-called Slansky Trials" (p. 5).

Two other modern purposes for torture emerged. **Interrogational torture** is integrally related to national security. Its purpose is to extract *actionable intelligence*, which means forward-looking information of security value. While interrogational torture certainly has been a feature of **conventional war**s (armed conflicts between or among states), it is especially common in **unconventional/asymmetric war**s (conflicts between states and non-state groups) and **civil war**s (armed conflicts within a country). The main rationale for interrogational torture is to extract from individuals information that would not otherwise be available, for example the names, plans, or hiding places of enemies who do not wear uniforms or possess heavy armaments like tanks and airplanes.

Terroristic torture describes rampant custodial violence in the context of state terror. Often it is coupled with **extra-judicial execution** (killing people without charge or trial). According to Henry Shue (2004: 53), the purpose of terroristic torture is "intimidation of persons other than the victim," for example to deter political opponents and raise the costs of resistance to the government. Terroristic torture is an *invisible spectacle* because people are made fearful of torture that they know is occurring but do not actually see themselves.

One of the most notable episodes of terroristic torture occurred in Cambodia in the seventies. When the Khmer Rouge came to power in 1975, they pursued the goal of turning the country into a purely agrarian-based communist society through a campaign of social engineering that included nationwide forced labor and depopulation of cities. During the four years they ruled the country, over three million people (in a population of seven million) died, many as a result of torture and extra-judicial execution (Bernstein 2009; Chandler 2000). The targeted enemies included intellectuals and professionals, urbanites, religious people (Christians, Buddhists, and Muslims), ethnic minorities (Vietnamese, Chinese, and Thai), people with ties to the previous regimes or foreign governments, and anyone suspected of harboring free market ideas. One of the Khmer Rouge's mottos was: "To keep you is no benefit. To destroy you is no loss."

Regime Types and Torture

Totalitarianism is a political system in which the state exercises total power over all aspects of society, and state terror is pervasive. The Soviet Union during Stalin's era and Nazi Germany are the archetypal models of totalitarian states. In *The Origins of Totalitarianism*, Hannah Arendt (1973: 453) explains that torture was "an essential feature of the whole totalitarian police and judiciary apparatus; it is used every day to make people talk." If you have read *1984* by George Orwell (1949) and are familiar with the concept of "Big Brother," you know what she means.

Authoritarianism describes regimes where state power is concentrated in the hands of a few political leaders and where repression is frequently used to maintain that power. Authoritarian regimes can take various forms, including military juntas, fascist or racist regimes, dictatorships, theocracies, and one-party states. What they share in common is an utter lack of accountability of the state to society. Torture is a common means for authoritarians to sustain their power, intimidate or destroy opponents, and/or reinforce the ruling ideology.

Colonialism is a form of rule where one country takes control of a conquered foreign territory and its population, and establishes a colony. The history of colonialism dates back to the 1500s when European governments began taking over and establishing their own rule throughout the Americas, Africa, and Asia. Horrific forms of violence were used to subdue, exploit, or exterminate indigenous populations (Fanon 2004; Hochschild 1999; Taussig 1984). By 1900, the height of *the age of empire*, 80 percent of the world's landmass was ruled by European states.

In the 20th century, colonial torture acquired a new purpose: to counter and combat anti-colonial resistance to European rule. In many colonies, people rose up to assert their right to **self-determination**—to rule themselves by establishing new national governments to replace colonial states. In many colonies, especially where resistance took the form of armed struggle, the use of torture intensified dramatically (Elkins 2005; Khalili 2012; Kramer 2008). In these conflicts, which pitted states against non-state groups, the latter were characterized as "insurgents," and the conflicts were depicted (from the perspective of the colonizers) as "counter-insurgency warfare." The rebels called them wars of liberation.

In 1931, French colonial police pioneered the use of electric torture to thwart nationalist resistance in Indochina, the colony that encompassed what is today Vietnam and Cambodia (Rejali 2007: 5). In the fifties, the French engaged in pervasive torture in Algeria to combat nationalist/anti-colonial resistance (Alleg 2006; Aussaresses 2002; Horne 1978; Lazreg 2008). French torture was immortalized in Gillo Pontecorvo's (1966) film *The Battle of Algiers*. Although some members of the Algerian National Liberation Front who were subjected to the French mix of water torture, electric shock, and beatings did divulge information and the French army won the Battle of Algiers, when revelations about the use of torture got back to France, it undermined public support for the war. France quit Algeria in 1962 and the country became independent. Thus, if torture's purpose was to sustain French control of that country, it failed.

Democracy is an ideal type of government because it means that the state truly *represents* the society it rules, and members of society—at least citizens—have an institutionalized opportunity to pick and change their leaders through elections and other lawful and peaceful means. In the real world, democratic government is never a perfect reflection of the will of the people, especially when societies are politically divided along racial, religious, ethnic, or other lines. Nevertheless, democratic governments tend to be committed to the rule of law because citizens *expect* their leaders and governing institutions to act legally and to defend and respect the rights of their people.

However, when democracies occupy foreign territories as a result of war or rule populations who aspire to political independence or a different form of government, they are not democratically representative *in those places*. When conflicts arise in such contexts, as they inevitably do, national security considerations tend to trump democratic principles. It is under these circumstances that democracies act like colonial states (because, in a way, they are), including the security-rationalized use of torture.

The French in Algeria exemplifies this, as does the U.S. record in militarily occupied Afghanistan and Iraq, as discussed in Chapter 1.

Cold War Torture

During World War II, the United States and the Soviet Union (USSR) put aside their hostilities to become allies in order to defeat Nazi Germany and the fascist regimes of Italy and Japan. However, after that war ended in 1945, a new kind of global war began: the Cold War. The opposing sides were the communist East, dominated by the USSR, and the capitalist West, dominated by the United States. This war was "cold" because there was no direct military confrontation—no hot war—between the world's two superpowers.

For the West, the goals and objectives of the Cold War were the *containment* of communism within the Eastern Bloc (countries in Eastern and Central Europe that fell under Soviet sway at the end of WWII), *rollback* of communism in other areas where it had gained a foothold, and the prevention of its spread elsewhere. When the Communist Party led by Mao Zedong took power in mainland China in 1949, Western fear of communist world domination intensified.

The Korean peninsula, which had been ruled by Imperial Japan since 1910, was divided along the 38th parallel at the end of WWII with the Soviets occupying the north and the United States occupying the south. In this regard, it was similar to the post-war division of Germany into East and West. A communist government was established in North Korea and a capitalist one was established in South Korea. The Korean War started in 1950 when the North invaded the South. The United States sent the military to fight on the side of the south. The Soviets did not directly intervene, but China joined the war on the side of the north. After three years, the war ended with a military stalemate and Korea remains divided. If you have seen Robert Altman's (1970) movie *M.A.S.H.*, or the spin-off TV show of the same name, you have some familiarity with this war.

One of the aspects of the Korean War was the terrible mistreatment of American **prisoners of war (POWs)**. Many soldiers who were captured by the North Koreans were beaten, starved, put into forced labor, marched to death, or summarily executed. China also committed war crimes against POWs, but added a new tactic to their repertoire of mistreatment: after starving prisoners into a weakened state, they subjected them to communist indoctrination. John Frankenheimer's (1962) political thriller *The Manchurian Candidate* features a character who was "brainwashed" to become an assassin for an international communist conspiracy. (After President John F. Kennedy was assassinated in 1963 the film was rarely shown for decades.)

The CIA took a lesson from the Korean War. Fearful that a communist regime might achieve a breakthrough in the art of brainwashing, in 1953 the Agency established the

MK-ULTRA program and invested in mind-control research. This began with experiments in hypnosis, electroshock, and hallucinogenic drugs. (LSD was invented by the CIA.) The CIA program evolved into **psychological torture**, which fuses tactics of sensory deprivation and self-inflicted pain (i.e. position abuse). Unlike beatings and other tactics that violently attack the body, this combination targets the mind and "causes victims to feel responsible for their suffering and thus capitulate more readily to their torturers" (McCoy 2006: 8). In 1963, the CIA produced *Kubark Counterintelligence Interrogation*, a manual for understanding and using various combinations of tactics that systematically attack all of the human senses to produce effects of "debility, disorientation and dread."

Hot Wars

Both sides in the Cold War competed to expand their spheres of influence throughout the Third World, also referred to as the Global South. Both superpowers engaged in political and military interventionism in many countries to try to influence the outcomes of anti-colonial struggles that were picking up steam in the fifties and sixties, as well as the economic policies and political alignments of newly independent countries. Those competitions spawned plenty of hot wars and, with it, plenty of torture.

In order to pursue the Cold War agenda of fighting communism, in 1946, the U.S. Defense Department established the **School of the Americas** in Panama to train military officials from South and Central American countries. The objective was to school students in counter-insurgency warfare and to indoctrinate them about the dangers of communism. In addition to conventional military training, the curriculum included commando operations and psychological warfare, how to be effective snipers, and the latest in interrogation techniques.

By the late 1950s, the United States viewed the conflict in Vietnam as critical to the Cold War goal of containment and rollback of communism. Vietnam was divided between a communist nationalist government controlling the North, and a non-communist government in the South. The United States started sending forces to South Vietnam in the early sixties. To root out Southern guerillas (Viet Cong) who were allied with the North, the CIA trained more than 85,000 South Vietnamese police, who operated a network of interrogational torture sites across the country. The CIA developed the Phoenix program, which typified terroristic torture in its combination of brutal inter-rogations and extra-judicial executions. The program was an intelligence-gathering failure, and more than 26,000 prisoners were either tortured to death or summarily executed, most of whom were almost certainly not Viet Cong (McCoy 2006: 68).

In 1959, Fidel Castro's forces won the revolutionary war in Cuba and installed a communist government allied to the USSR. American anxieties about the spread of communism in the Western hemisphere dictated foreign and military policy for decades.

The counter-insurgency warfare models honed in Vietnam were transported to Latin America in the sixties through Project X, a secret training program of Army Intelligence for militaries and police. The Phoenix program model was incorporated into the curriculum of the School of the Americas.

Reigns of State Terror in Latin America

Although most South American countries had gained political independence by the 19th century, in the mid-20th century the rising discourse of anti-imperialism in Africa and Asia inspired leaders of some countries to try to break free of the neo-imperial grip of a global economy dominated by the West—or, in this case, the North. These leaders believed that their own economic dependency could be transformed into development by nationalizing important industries that were run or dominated by foreign-based multinational corporations, and by delinking national economies from the global capitalist market for a period of time in order to build their own capacities to become industrial competitors rather than producers of cheap raw materials. To do so, they adopted the Import–Substitution–Industrialization (ISI) model. At first, this ISI model was an engine for economic growth as countries produced their own steel, cars, televisions, and other products. But national markets were not big enough to sustain demand for nationally manufactured goods. As this ISI model began to fail in country after country, right-wing military leaders seized power from democratically elected governments, with U.S. encouragement and assistance. Their initial goal was to reinsert those economies back into the global capitalist market.

Through the School of the Americas and other U.S. institutions (including the philanthropic Ford Foundation), Latin American military and political leaders were educated about the free market theories of Milton Friedman, an economics professor at the University of Chicago. Friedman and his acolytes, nicknamed the Chicago Boys, were opposed to any state involvement in the economy. They believed that for the market to be truly "free," government regulation of industry, subsidies, and social welfare programs should end. The Chicago Boys argued that everything about the economy should be privatized and opened up to free market competition.

What, you might wonder, does this have to do with torture? In *The Shock Doctrine*, Naomi Klein (2007) explains how Friedman's fascination with the fifties CIA-funded research into electric shock therapy to turn individuals' minds into empty slates that could be inscribed with new information (brainwashing) inspired his theories about how whole societies could be shocked to accept (unpopular) free market policies of privatization, deregulation, and the termination of social programs. In 1973, Friedman advised Chilean dictator Augusto Pinochet, who had just seized power (with U.S. assistance) from the democratically elected president, Salvador Allende, to impose economic shock therapy while Chilean society was in shock from the coup. Thus,

Chile became the first place where the Chicago Boys' theories could be applied in the real world.

Those economic shock policies instituted by the Pinochet regime and emulated by other Latin American military dictatorships were a disaster. In the short term, the gutting of public services and popular social welfare programs (like cheap tuition for college) sparked unrest as people protested the declining standards of living. Over the longer term, national revenues diminished as multinational corporations bought up de-nationalized industries and transported profits to shareholders abroad. To defend their policies and subdue unrest, these military regimes embarked on national wars against domestic subversives and enemies, which they regarded as part of the West's war against international communism.

In these "dirty wars," the people targeted by the region's military regimes were depicted as traitors and communists, or guilty by association to leftist political movements. As Lawrence Weschler explains, the doctrine of national security guiding these military regimes was "a fearsome piece of work. ... The enemy—the International Communist Movement—is perceived as covertly operating everywhere, all the time, in all fields of human endeavor" (1998: 121).

Terroristic torture was rampant in Latin America from the sixties through the eighties (Feitlowitz 1998; Kornbluh 2003; Langguth 1979). The word "**disappeared**" was given a new meaning (to be disappeared) to describe how people who were arrested were killed after they were tortured, and their bodies were disposed of in ways that meant they could never be found again. One method of disappearing people was to take them in military helicopters over the ocean, cut open their stomachs and place rocks inside so that their bodies would sink when they were thrown out.

All of the region's U.S.-backed military regimes perpetrated torture. But its uses varied from country to country. In Brazil, the first country where the military seized power (in 1961), 23 political prisoners were prosecuted in security courts for every one who was extra-judicially executed. In Chile, the ratio was 1.5 to one. In Argentina, only one person was tried for every 71 who were disappeared—the fate of approximately 30,000 people (Pereira 2008). Uruguay had the highest per capita torture and incarceration rate in the world during the period of military rule; one in every 50 citizens was interrogated by torture, and one in every 500 received a long prison sentence for political offenses (Weschler 1998: 88).

Although it is impossible to know exactly how many people were tortured by these Latin American military regimes, experts estimate the number between 100,000 and 150,000, tens of thousands of whom were killed (Klein 2007: 95). To contemplate whether torture *worked*, we should consider the fates of the regimes: Most abandoned or were driven from power by the late eighties. In some countries, their records became the subject of investigations and published reports that took as their titles "never again" (*nunca más* in Spanish, *nunca mais* in Portuguese—the language of Brazil). The concept of "never again" is a signal of their abject failures.

The military regimes had granted themselves immunity for any crimes they committed while they were in power. However, with the passage of time and changing political environments, demands for legal accountability for crimes of state began to build. Since 1990, a number of leaders of the former military regimes have faced prosecution for torture and other crimes (Lutz and Reiger 2009). In Chapter 5, I discuss the fate of Pinochet because it altered the legal liability for torture on an international scale.

When Democracies Torture

The long-running conflict in Northern Ireland was one context where a democracy, Britain, used torture on suspected members of the Irish Republican Army (IRA). For centuries, the British had dominated Ireland where the population was Catholic, and facilitated the settlement of English Protestants. The countries of the British Isles (England, Scotland, Wales, and Ireland) formed one sovereign unit: the United Kingdom (UK). The Irish struggle for independence, which picked up in the early 20th century, was opposed by many Protestants, who were concentrated in the north. They wanted to retain the union, hence they called themselves Unionists. Following a period of warring between the IRA and British forces, a peace treaty was signed and Ireland was split in 1922. Northern Ireland remained part of the UK.

In the late 1960s, a new period of violent clashes and bloody riots erupted in Northern Ireland, which was termed "the troubles." The IRA and Protestant paramilitary groups attacked each other and carried out bombings and other acts of terrorism directed at civilians of the other side. British soldiers were brought in to restore order. The British use of armed force against Irish civilians, including the notorious Bloody Sunday massacre, elevated popular support for the IRA among Northern Irish nationalists. In their effort to gather information about IRA operations and networks, British interrogators employed *five techniques*: wall standing, hooding, subjection to noise, sleep deprivation, and deprivation of food and drink (see Feldman 1991).

Did those techniques constitute torture? That was the question put before the European Court of Human Rights (ECHR) when the Republic of Ireland brought a case challenging the five techniques as a violation of European law (*Ireland* v. *United Kingdom*). In the ECHR's 1978 decision (13 to 4), the majority ruled that those techniques do not rise to the level of "torture" but they do constitute "inhumane and degrading treatment," which is also prohibited. The British government, however, accepted the minority opinion that the techniques constitute (or come close to) torture, especially when used in combination, and decided to forego their use.

Israel, also a democracy, has been in a continuing state of war since a sovereign Jewish state was established in 1948 over 70 percent of what previously had been the British-controlled Palestine Mandate. During the 1948–49 war, more than 700,000

Palestinians fled or were expelled from areas that became part of Israel, many of whom became refugees in surrounding Arab countries. Palestinians who remained inside Israel became citizens, although they did not enjoy equal rights and were governed by a military administration until 1966. The remaining parts of Palestine did not become a separate independent state. Rather, Jordan took control of the West Bank and Egypt took control of the Gaza Strip. In 1964, the Palestine Liberation Organization (PLO) was established as the national representative of the Palestinian people. Headquartered in the diaspora, the PLO's mandate was to lead the fight for Palestinian statehood.

In the 1967 Arab–Israeli War, Israel defeated the surrounding states in six days and captured the West Bank and the Gaza Strip. Israel did not assert sovereignty but rather established a military administration to govern Palestinians residing in the occupied territories. An important part of this administration is the Israeli military court system. This system has been used to prosecute Palestinians suspected of violating Israel's military and emergency laws, which criminalize not only acts of violence, sabotage, and militancy but also membership of local factions associated with the PLO and a vast array of political and non-violent activities. Israel relied on prosecution as one of its key strategies to control the West Bank and Gaza and to thwart and punish Palestinian nationalist resistance to the occupation. In the vast majority of military court cases, people have been convicted and imprisoned on the basis of confessions (Hajjar 2005).

For two decades, allegations that interrogators working for Israel's General Security Service (GSS) tortured Palestinian detainees for confessions and intelligence were consistently denied by government officials as lies and fabrications of "enemies of the state." Then in 1987 (for reasons unconnected to the interrogation of Palestinians), the Israeli government established an official commission of inquiry to investigate the GSS. The Landau Commission confirmed that GSS agents *had* used violent interrogation methods on Palestinian detainees since at least 1971, contrary to official denials, and that those agents had routinely lied when confessions were challenged in court on the grounds that they had been coerced. The Landau Commission was harsh in its criticism of GSS perjury (i.e. lying to military judges), but adopted the GSS's own position that coercive interrogation tactics were *necessary* in the struggle against "hostile terrorist activity." The Landau Commission adopted a broad definition of terrorism to encompass not only acts or threats of violence, but all activities related to Palestinian nationalism.

The Landau Commission report concluded that the defense of Israeli national security requires physical and psychological coercion in the interrogation of Palestinians, and recommended that the state should sanction such tactics in order to alleviate the problem of perjury. The Landau Commission's justification for this recommendation was based on a three-part contention: that Palestinians have forfeited their right not to be abusively interrogated because of their predisposition for terrorism, that the GSS

Figure 3.1 Israeli interrogators routinely used hooding, stress positions, and painful cuffing.
Source: David Gerstein; used by permission.

operates morally and responsibly in discharging its duties to defend Israeli national security, and that GSS interrogation methods do not constitute "torture." The Landau Commission sought to avoid the scourge of the torture label by euphemizing the endorsed tactics as "**moderate physical pressure**."

The Landau Commission's reasoning that "moderate physical pressure" does not constitute "torture" traces back to British interrogation methods used on IRA prisoners. The Commission noted that Israeli interrogation tactics resembled the five techniques, and embraced the ECHR's majority decision that they do not rise to the level of torture. These tactics include stress positions, protracted sleep deprivation, isolation, prolonged hooding, sensory manipulation (e.g. excruciatingly loud noise), and painful cuffing.

In November 1987, the Israeli government accepted the Landau Commission's recommendations and officially authorized "moderate physical pressure." Thus Israel became the first state in the modern world to *publicly* endorse the use of painful, degrading, and inhumane interrogation techniques as a "legal right" of the state.

The timing of this license to torture was unpropitious because in December 1987, Palestinians started an *intifada* (uprising) to protest the continuing occupation. This mass movement was, initially, unarmed. Israel responded with armed force as well as a massive increase in arrests, interrogations, and prosecutions through the military courts. At the end of the 1980s, Israel had the highest per capita prison population in the world.

In the early 1990s, Palestinian Islamists affiliated with Hamas and Islamic Jihad, which were political competitors with the more secular PLO, began using the tactic of suicide bombing, sometimes as reprisals for Israeli assassination operations. In response to the heightened insecurity caused by such bombings, Israeli interrogational torture increased. However, contrary to the hypothetical ticking bomb scenario (see Chapter 1), which the Landau Commission had invoked in arguing the necessity of abuse, there has never been a documented instance of an *actual* ticking bomb (i.e. one that is imminently set to explode) that was discovered and defused through torture. Rather, in Israeli national security discourse, Palestinian resistance to the occupation—both violent and non-violent—*is* the ticking bomb.

In response to the Israeli government's authorization of tactics and treatment widely regarded as torture, some Israeli and Palestinian lawyers and human rights activists waged a decade-long battle in Israeli courts to end the use of "moderate physical pressure." Those efforts ultimately were victorious when, in 1999, the Israeli High Court of Justice ruled that the "routine" abuse of detainees was unacceptable and prohibited. Israeli interrogational abuse of prisoners did not stop completely (PCATI 2003), but that court decision deprived it of the veneer of legality.

Ironically, the Israeli model of "legalizing" torture as necessary in the fight against terrorism was influential for the authors of the U.S. "torture memos" (see Chapter 1), but not the court decision that ruled against the routine and systematic use of abusive techniques.

DISCUSSION QUESTIONS

1. Many modern states use torture. What are some of the common reasons they do so, and what difference does **regime type** make in understanding this phenomenon?
2. Torture often occurs in the context of war. Identify one war featured in this chapter, and discuss why and how torture was utilized.
3. In the modern era, torture techniques were devised to target the "mind" (i.e. psyche, personality) although many of these techniques also involved physical methods (e.g. stress positions). Thinking broadly about political transformations and conflicts in the modern era, discuss why the mind became a target.

IV: Torture and Rights

⌒⌒⌒

This chapter explores the relationship between rights and law, including **human rights** and international law. In the preface, I wrote that the right not to be tortured is the most universal right that human beings have. In this chapter I explain what that means and elaborate on the importance of the right not to be tortured.

Understanding Rights

To understand how rights *work*, we need a very clear definition of what rights *are*. Here is my definition: **Rights** *are practices that are required, prohibited, or otherwise regulated in the context of relationships governed by law.*

To unpack this definition, we begin with the point that *rights are practices*. I was inspired by the work of Michel Foucault (1990), who argues that "power" is not a thing that one owns, but rather it exists and functions as practices in relations among people and institutions. People *exercise* power; they don't own power. The same applies to rights, which are not things that one owns like a book or a pair of shoes, but rather they work through practices among people and institutions. For example, the *right* to vote is not the act of casting a vote, but rather it is composed of the practices that are required or are prohibited in order to enable people to vote. Having this right obligates the state to engage in a variety of practices, including registering voters, providing police protection so voters can safely access the polling places on voting day, and establishing impartial means to count ballots.

The second part of the definition, that rights are practices that *are required, prohibited, or otherwise regulated ... by law*, distinguishes rights from other types of practices. Rights are legal entitlements that are created through laws. For example, breathing is a practice but not a right. We don't have a law to guarantee our right to breathe because breathing as a routine human function is not at risk under normal circumstances. However, when a person's ability to breathe is purposefully thwarted—for example, if someone is suffocated during interrogation—the right to breathe in that context is constituted through the laws providing the right not to be tortured. The words "required" and "prohibited" tell us something about how rights work: Those that require certain kinds of practices are **positive rights** because they grant *freedom to* something, such as the vote, education, or self-determination. Those that prohibit certain kinds of practices, such as torture or racial discrimination, are **negative rights** because they involve *freedom from* something that is legally prohibited. People *have* such rights because *there is no legal right to do those prohibited things.*

The third part of the definition, that rights are practices that are required, prohibited, or otherwise regulated *in the context of relationship governed by law*, refers to the kinds of people and relationships that are covered by a law's jurisdiction. For example, neither children who *are* U.S. citizens nor adults who are *not* U.S. citizens have the right to vote in American elections because they are excluded from the jurisdiction of voting laws. When citizens turn 18, they acquire the right to vote because they have a new identity as adults, and this qualifies them to participate in the selection of their political representatives. History is full of examples of formerly unregulated relations that were brought "into the law" through legal reform or innovation. For example, until the early seventies, in the United States and elsewhere the (non-deadly) abuse of one family member by another was legally unregulated, and thus there was no "right" not to be beaten or tormented by a spouse, parent, or sibling in the home. It was not that the law had nothing to say about such (domestic) violence. Rather, what the law said was that it would not enter the house to intervene because domestic relations were regarded as "private" and therefore not the state's or the law's business. That was unacceptable to feminists and anti-violence activists. They wanted the law to go into the house to protect people there. They generated political pressure to bring domestic violence into the law by persuading law makers (legislators) to criminalize these types of practice, and this created new rights for people to be safe from violence in domestic settings, including the right to seek the aid of the police if they were beaten or abused. Having the right not to be domestically abused obligates the state to engage in practices to prevent such harms, to protect victims, and to punish perpetrators.

One of the common misperceptions about rights is that if the laws are violated and those violations are ignored or unenforced, then people don't "have" rights. We need to understand the distinction among *getting rights*, which occurs when demands for rights are realized through the creation of new laws or the extension of existing laws to new subjects (e.g. when the voting age in America was changed from 21 to 18, younger people *got* the right to vote); *enjoying rights*, which means actually experiencing the protections, freedoms, and opportunities that rights laws promise; and *having rights*, which refers to a right to rights, whether or not the laws are effectively enforced. To (mistakenly) think that people only *have* the rights that they *enjoy* is to presume that the law serves no function if it is not respected and enforced. But this would be analogous to saying that criminal law serves no function if some crimes that are committed go unpunished. That is an obvious absurdity. The same holds true for rights laws.

What Good Are Rights?

The importance of rights is the subject of fascinating and wide-ranging intellectual debates (see Nielsen 2004). These include various skeptical interpretations. For example,

Stuart Scheingold's (2004) work on "the myth of rights" argues that when people pursue their rights by going to court, they are engaging in a mythic belief that judges have the power and the inclination to make the world a better place for them. His point is that rights are better protected through political work to make respect for those rights popular to society. Kristin Bumiller's (1988) study of the "civil rights society" addresses the fact that the legal protection model of anti-discrimination law requires people who have been discriminated against to comport themselves like victims and to participate in law enforcement processes. However, some people—especially those who are socially disadvantaged by race, gender, or class—either cannot or do not want to take on the identity of a victim and initiate legal action against their discriminators. Therefore, Bumiller argues, anti-discrimination law is not an effective tool for guaranteeing their rights. Scholars associated with Critical Legal Studies advanced a *critique of rights* along the lines that "the master's tools will not dismantle the master's house." This critique is premised on the idea that law tends to be interpreted and enforced to support the status quo, and therefore relying on law reinforces hierarchies of social power (Galanter 1974; Gordon 1998; Rosenberg 1991).

The critique of rights gave rise to the *critique of the critique of rights*. Scholars associated with Critical Race Theory (Crenshaw, et al. 1995; Williams 1991) have argued that even though law is not always or even often responsive to the rights claims of minorities and socially vulnerable populations, nevertheless *having* legal rights is important because it provides a way of making certain demands on the state and society to provide justice, equality, and fair treatment. Without the law, those demands would be "just politics," subject to the will and whim of discriminating majorities. Kimberle Crenshaw (1995: 111) explains that the value of rights "is precisely this legitimating function that has made law receptive to certain demands in this area."

I agree with the critique of the critique of rights and, as I explain below, it is even *more* relevant to international human rights. But there are two additional reasons why *having* rights are important. First, laws that establish and define rights constitute standards against which conditions and relations in the real world can be assessed and judged. Rights laws transform practices that were once merely "bad" or "harmful," for example domestic violence or denial of the right to vote, into *legal violations*. In this regard, rights law is a powerful language and resource for condemnation of the range of harms that constitute rights violations.

The second reason I believe having rights is important is more idiosyncratic in the sense that it is not very well developed in scholarship on rights. Rights are valuable not just because they have the capacity or promise to make the world a better place by offering protections and freedoms that *help people* live more dignified and safe lives. Rights also have the underappreciated (and still underdeveloped) capacity to *hurt perpetrators* who violate rights laws. The enforcement of rights laws whose violations are crimes (like torture) involves prosecuting and punishing perpetrators. Some scholars who write about rights do not like to think of rights-law enforcement as a form of legal harm. But prosecution and punishment through the enforcement of criminal law is a form of *retributive justice* because perpetrators are made to pay retribution—*to suffer for their crimes*. Punishment also is intended to be a *deterrent* against future crimes by persuading or scaring potential violators of the consequences they will face if they disregard and break the law.

Here is the idiosyncratic part of my argument: when it comes to the right not to be tortured, the violation of which is a very serious crime—albeit distinguished from many other crimes by the fact that it is often perpetrated by state agents or people acting on behalf of a state—there should be more popular support and enthusiasm for the vengeful "tough on crime" sentiments that are popular in terms of other kinds of crime. If you can understand that murderers should be punished, how hard is it to understand that torturers should be punished? Such punishment is a necessary component of the defense of the right not to be tortured.

The Creation of Human Rights

Like other kinds of rights, human rights are legal entitlements. These rights, however, are created through international laws and extend to all human beings *as such*. In the span of history, human rights are relatively new. Although the idea of human rights was in circulation over the last few centuries, there was no such thing as international human rights law prior to the end of World War II. Previously, whatever rights humans *had* were provided through national and other kinds of local law, and international laws were oriented mainly to the rights of sovereign states and relations among states. Why did that change?

World War II was a "total war" because the opposing sides attacked not only each other's militaries but also set out to destroy civilians in unprecedented ways. In World War II, 50 percent of the tens of millions killed were civilians, whereas in World War I, the proportion of civilian deaths was 10 percent. The strategies and consequences of World War II included firebombing and atomic bombing cities, massive rape, enslavement, and ethnic cleansings (mass expulsions and massacres). Arguably the most revolting campaign was the Nazi Holocaust in which millions of people—Jews, communists, homosexuals, Roma, and others—were systematically exterminated by the German government. The grimmest lesson of the war was that some of the most egregious atrocities were not *illegal* because there were no laws to prohibit them and no authority to prevent them.

At the end of World War II, new legal ground was broken when the victorious Allies (the United States, the USSR, and Britain) established the **Nuremberg and Tokyo Tribunals** to try leaders from the defeated states of Germany and Japan. The prosecution of individuals for crimes that they had perpetrated as government officials upended the sovereign prerogative of states to use violence with impunity in areas they controlled. Hermann Goering, one of the architects of the Nazi "Final Solution" to exterminate the Jews of Europe, challenged the idea that what he and his government had done was a crime. He said, "But that was our right! We were a sovereign state and that was strictly our business." As a matter of law, he was actually correct. But the Holocaust provided the *negative inspiration* for the international community *to change the law* in order to prevent in the future what had happened in the immediate past. One change was the invention of **crimes against humanity**, which refers to large-scale and/or systematic attacks on civilians and civilian infrastructure, whether occurring in war or peace.

In his opening statement as lead prosecutor at the Nuremberg Tribunal, U.S. Supreme Court Justice Robert Jackson said:

> If these men are the first leaders of a defeated nation to be prosecuted in the name of the law, they are also the first to be given a chance to plead for their lives in the name of the law … a favor which these men, when in power, rarely extended to their fellow countrymen. Despite the fact that public opinion already condemns their acts, we agree that here they must be given a presumption of innocence, and we accept the burden of proving [their] criminal acts.

The principles justifying the prosecution of Axis leaders were lofty and new: The defendants were being tried for crimes against "humanity" and "peace," not against particular victims of their regimes. The concept of sovereign immunity was rejected as a legal defense because defendants were not excused for their own heinous actions by claiming that they were just "following orders" of commanding officers and civilian leaders. *Individuals* who exercised the sovereign power of states were held criminally accountable for crimes of states.

In addition to the tribunals, the two most significant post-war initiatives to build a new international regime were the establishment of the **United Nations (UN)** in 1945, and the passage of the **Universal Declaration of Human Rights (UDHR)** in 1948. The UN was created to provide a forum where representatives of all sovereign states could meet and collaborate to ensure the common good of global peace and security. The UDHR was a high-minded document that sought to establish "a common standard of achievement for all peoples and all nations," and declared that all humans had certain "inalienable rights." You should check out the UDHR to see the spectrum of issues that constitute human rights (http://www.un.org/en/documents/udhr).

Although the UDHR was a non-binding agreement (i.e. a declaration is not a law), it laid out a framework for a common and collective ("universal" and "indivisible") set of rights that all humans could claim, and it served as a reference for subsequent efforts to transform those principles into actual international laws. Article 5 of the UDHR states: "No one shall be subjected to torture or to cruel, inhuman or degrading treatment or punishment."

Given the significance of the Nazi Holocaust as a motivation for the creation of human rights, it should not be surprising that **genocide** was the subject of the first human rights law. The **Genocide Convention**, passed by the UN in 1948, classified it as a crime whether it occurred in war or peace. But the definition was limited to efforts intended "to destroy, in whole or in part, a national, ethnical [ethnic], racial or religious group, as such." The exclusion of "political groups" and the insertion of the phrase "as such" were insisted upon by the major powers to preserve their own prerogatives to perpetrate violence against political enemies.

The other major post-war innovation was in the area of international humanitarian law (IHL). Unlike human rights law, which was new, IHL dates back to the late 19th century when the millennia-old customary laws of war were injected with humanitarian concerns to minimize *unnecessary* suffering and *excessive* violence and inhumane treatment. The laws of war were divided into two bodies: "Hague laws," which regulate what is permissible and prohibited between belligerents engaged in armed conflict, and "Geneva laws," which embodied the new spirit of humanitarianism. The first Geneva Convention (1864) established an obligation not to abandon wounded soldiers to die on the battlefield. World War I provided the negative inspiration for the Geneva Protocol of 1925 prohibiting the use of asphyxiating, poisonous, and bacteriological weapons, as well as the 1929 Geneva Convention expanding rules for the treatment of wounded, sick, and captured soldiers.

The four Geneva Conventions of 1949 refined and innovated key rules and principles of IHL, namely *civilian immunity* (i.e. the prohibition against deliberately targeting civilians and other non-combatants or otherwise treating them as combatants); *distinction* (i.e. the imperative to distinguish between civilians and combatants, and for combatants to distinguish themselves as such by wearing uniforms and carrying arms openly); *proportionality* (i.e. the injunction to limit the use of force in a way that it is proportional—not excessive—to the military value of the target); *necessity* (i.e. the imperative to restrict targets or tactics to those necessary to achieve legitimate military goals); and *humane treatment* (i.e. positive duties on custodians of war prisoners and those ruling civilians in militarily occupied territories). Serious violations (grave breaches) of the Geneva Conventions are **war crimes**. These include torture as well as forced relocations and deportations, collective punishment, hostage-taking, and extra-judicial killings.

These developments in international law to expand the rights of humans in war or peace did not undermine the centrality of sovereign states to political life around the world. Rather, they created new *internationalized norms of government* to which all states would be expected to adhere, while preserving states' rights as sovereign entities. Consequently, while states' rights were revised (e.g. they could no longer claim the "right" to exterminate civilians), states retained their status as the premiere subjects of international law. Put simply, human rights obtained their "universalizing" character from the fact that people are subjects of states, and states are subjects of international law. Thus the establishment of human rights and the elaboration of humanitarian rules for warfare simultaneously altered and reinforced the power of states in the international order because states are the governors and the governed—the makers, the enforcers, and the subjects of international laws.

The greatest weakness in this new legal regime was the refusal by powerful states—including the United States—to establish an institution capable of enforcing international law. Plans were shelved to establish a permanent international criminal court modeled on the Nuremberg and Tokyo Tribunals. Hence, human beings' abilities to *enjoy* their human rights depended on whether the state under whose authority they lived was willing to self-enforce these laws.

At the end of the forties, the development of human rights was frozen by the Cold War until the sixties when many formerly colonized countries achieved their national independence, which changed the composition of the UN. The second human rights law, passed in 1965, was the Convention on the Elimination of All Forms of Racial Discrimination. The enduring communist–capitalist polarities of the Cold War were reflected in the inability of the UN to pass a single International Bill of Rights that would enshrine all the rights in the UDHR. Instead, in 1966 two separate laws were passed: the International Covenant on Economic, Social and Cultural Rights (ICESCR), and the International Covenant on Civil and Political Rights (ICCPR). The United States never ratified the ICESCR because officials regard these rights, such as to food, housing, and equal pay for equal work, to smack of socialism and contradict the principles of free market capitalism.

Understanding the Human Right Not To Be Tortured

Although torture was prohibited under the UDHR, the Geneva Conventions, and the ICCPR, it was not until 1984 when the UN passed the Convention against Torture and Other Cruel, Inhuman, or Degrading Treatment or Punishment (CAT). According to Article 1, torture is defined as:

> any act by which severe pain or suffering, whether physical or mental, is intentionally inflicted on a person for such purposes as obtaining from him or a third person information or a confession, punishing him for an act he or a third person has committed or is suspected of having committed, or intimidating or coercing him or a third person, or for any reason based on discrimination of any kind, when such pain or suffering is inflicted by or at the instigation of or with the consent or acquiescence of a public official or other person acting in an official capacity. It does not include pain or suffering arising only from, inherent in or incidental to lawful sanctions.

Two factors distinguish torture from other types of violent and abusive things that people do to other people in face-to-face interactions. First, the law prohibits harms perpetrated against someone who is *in custody*—unfree to fight back or protect himself or herself and imperiled by that incapacitation. There are many circumstances when a person might be confined and vulnerable, but custody has a public character. For example, if someone is kidnapped by a criminal, that person is unfree, but the kidnapper is not a public agent and therefore the victim is not "in custody." Second, the prohibition of torture pertains to specific (and limited) motivations for the infliction of pain or suffering. Many kinds of harmful practices might "look like" torture, such as domestic violence, assault and battery, or even sadomasochistic sex, but they are not motivated by the purposes that constitute the international legal prohibition of torture.

Legally, severe pain and suffering constitute torture only if they are perpetrated against a person who is in custody by a person or people acting on behalf of some public authority or in an official capacity. This obviously applies to states and their agents, but it also could include non-state groups that exercise public power. For example, if a rebel group controls a certain area and has the capacity to capture and confine people, and then harms those captives for a purpose that serves the interests of the group, this would fit the meaning of torture.

The most contentious issue in contemporary debates about torture is where to draw the line between torture and the other category of harms referred to as **cruel, inhumane, and degrading treatment**. Because torture is categorically illegal and criminal, officials have an interest in denying that they engage in or authorize torture in order to avoid the label of torturer and the consequences that can arise. Below, I explain how the "politics of denial" works.

Frail Human Bodies and Core International Crimes

Human beings around the world live under vastly different conditions, including varied cultures, religions, economies, and political systems. But there are two things that all humans have in common: Everyone on earth has a *frail human body* that is capable of being damaged or destroyed by violence (Turner 1993, 2006; see also Butler 2004). And everyone is affected by state power because the world remains controlled and dominated by states. The impetus to create human rights was a desire to protect human frailty from the vicissitudes of state violence.

The right not to be tortured, along with the rights not to be subjected to genocide, war crimes, and crimes against humanity, have been termed the "'harder' human rights" (Hagan, Schoenfeld and Pallore 2006: 330) because they relate *directly* to the universality of the frail human body and often are perpetrated by states. Torture, genocide, war crimes, and crimes against humanity form a particularly serious class of violations: they are **core crimes under international law**. Four essential and common elements characterize these core crimes: They are all (*a*) forms of political violence that are (*b*) intentionally (*c*) perpetrated by people acting in a public capacity for public, not private, purposes (*d*) against captive or otherwise defenseless people.

What is distinctive about torture as both a violation of human rights and a war crime (if it occurs in the context of war) is the power and scope of the legal prohibition. The right not to be tortured extends to every human being regardless of any aspect of his or her identity. In contrast, even the right not to be genocidally exterminated depends on whether the perpetrators' intent to "destroy" people was motivated by specific (and limited) kinds of identity. Likewise, the kinds of activity defined as war crimes distinguish between soldiers and civilians; it is not a crime to kill soldiers in battle, and it is not even a crime to kill civilians if they are not targeted on purpose. The accidental (non-intentional) killing of civilians is referred to as "collateral damage." Thus, the right not to be tortured is stronger and more universal than the right to life because there are absolutely no exceptions, including in war and conflict, whereas there are many circumstances in which killing people is not illegal.

Human Rights Activism

Laws don't enforce themselves. This problem is particularly acute when it comes to international laws because there is no global government. Ideally, states enforce and abide by international laws. But this ideal is often breached, as detailed in Chapter 3. In order to promote the goal of international law enforcement, **human rights organizations** were established to strive to close the "gap" between laws in the books that establish humans' right to rights, and law in action through which people would be able to enjoy those rights.

Torture was the break-out issue for the development of an international **human rights movement**. Amnesty International, the "granddaddy" of human rights organizations, was formed in 1961 to combat torture and ill treatment, and the arrest of people for their political ideas and activities; those who endorsed non-violence were championed as "prisoners of conscience." Amnesty International devised a unique approach to **human rights activism**. It developed as a membership organization with chapters in many countries. In order to educate people around the world about human rights violations and to get them directly involved, Amnesty devised a strategy to disseminate information to members about individuals whose rights are being violated, along with information about how members could communicate their protest to the responsible government. By putting a "human face" to these messages, the aim was to elicit empathy for the suffering of strangers, to raise people's human rights consciousness, and to recruit the help of concerned people to close the gap between law in the books and law in action.

Since the seventies, human rights organizations have mushroomed around the world. Big ones like Human Rights Watch focus on a wide variety of violations anywhere they might occur. Others have mandates that focus on specific issues or categories (e.g. rights of women, children, native peoples, refugees). Some concentrate their work locally, others nationally, and others regionally.

Human rights activism takes various forms. But there are certain common strategies that organizations use to pursue the shared goal of closing the gap. These include *monitoring* to investigate and document violations, for example, taking testimonials from victims or witnesses; *reporting* on those violations to make that information public through human rights reports or media campaigns; *advocacy* work to lobby and pressure the UN or governments to take action to stop violations; and *litigation* to try to enforce international laws through courts.

The net effect of this institution building and activism since the seventies has raised awareness of human rights and has brought facts and analysis about violations into the public domain where they demand and command an audience. While violations are rampant in many countries, nevertheless, international human rights law provides a standard to judge the world and a language to condemn those who commit violations, and activism is the means to do so.

The Paradox of Torture

The **paradox of torture**, in a nutshell, is that it is both absolutely illegal and very pervasive. According to Professor Manfred Nowak, the UN Special Rapporteur on Torture from 2004 to 2010, "Torture is practiced in more than 90 percent of all countries in all regions of the world; big or small, dictatorship or democracy."

However, because of the universal illegality of torture, no government publicly acknowledges its own torture *as torture*. If we were to accept government rhetoric at face value, there is no torture in the world. How do regimes that use torture get away with such bald-faced lies? To some extent, it is a lot harder now than it used to be because human rights organizations have become increasingly effective at documenting and reporting on the use of torture.

Stanley Cohen (2001) addresses the paradox of torture and other gross violations by analyzing the **politics of denial**. Regimes that violate human rights are compelled to deny their wrongdoing in order to defend their reputations and avoid consequences. Such denials follow three common patterns. Sometimes it takes the form of **literal denial** when officials refute evidence with false proclamations that "we don't torture." Literal denial is a way of asking the world to believe *them* rather than those prisoners who claim they were tortured. If the evidence of torture is too clear or too well substantiated to be effectively denied with literal lies, or if a government wants to avoid the label of torture without actually altering its tactics and treatment of prisoners, officials engage in **interpretative denial**, for example using euphemisms to insist that authorized tactics are not torture but something else, like "moderate physical pressure" or "enhanced interrogation methods." The third form is **implicatory denial** in which a government might admit that torture occurred but blames it on (i.e. implicates) rogues, for example referring to them as "bad apples." Implicatory denial aims to shield higher officials from responsibility by denying that torture was authorized by people up the chain of command.

American officials engaged in all three kinds of denial when evidence of torture became public, as discussed in Chapter 1.

DISCUSSION QUESTIONS

1. What is the right not to be tortured, and how does it compare to other rights?
2. Examine the Universal Declaration of Human Rights and then discuss which of those human rights people in the United States do and do not "enjoy."
3. Human rights activism is a way for people anywhere in the world to work to close the gap between international laws in the books and law in action. Would you devote your energy to this kind of work? Explain your answer.

V: Enforcing the Right Not To Be Tortured

꙳꙳꙳

Torture is a core crime under international law, as explained in the previous chapter. In this chapter, I discuss efforts over the last two decades to hold perpetrators accountable.

International Criminal Law

In the late eighties and early nineties, several important events occurred on the international level that transformed the enforceability of **international criminal law** (i.e. the laws that criminalize torture, war crimes, crimes against humanity, and genocide). Those events were preceded by the collapse of the Soviet Union and communist or socialist regimes throughout Eastern and Central Europe, which brought the Cold War to an end. Other events occurring around this time included the end of apartheid in South Africa and transitions from military governments to civilian rule in Latin America and some other countries.

The optimism of a "new world order" following the end of the Cold War was short-lived when violence reminiscent of World War II erupted in Rwanda and the former Yugoslavia. In Rwanda, this took the form of genocide in which approximately 800,000 people were massacred in 100 days during 1994. In 1992, the multi-ethnic socialist state of Yugoslavia broke apart as different regions dominated by particular national and ethnic groups asserted their right to create sovereign states of their own. This led, in some parts of the former Yugoslavia, to wars, ethnic cleansings, and concentration camps where torture, rape, and murder were rampant.

As was the case at the end of World War II in which extreme violence was the negative inspiration for the creation of human rights, extreme violence in Rwanda and the former Yugoslavia was the negative inspiration that led to the creation of new institutions to enforce the laws that protect human rights. The end of the Cold War provided an opportunity to do so. The United Nations established ad hoc tribunals for the former Yugoslavia (in 1993) and Rwanda (in 1994) to prosecute the perpetrators of serious violations in those countries. These tribunals were the first *international* effort to recuperate the Nuremberg and Tokyo Tribunal model of holding individuals accountable for core crimes. Through the work of these tribunals, international

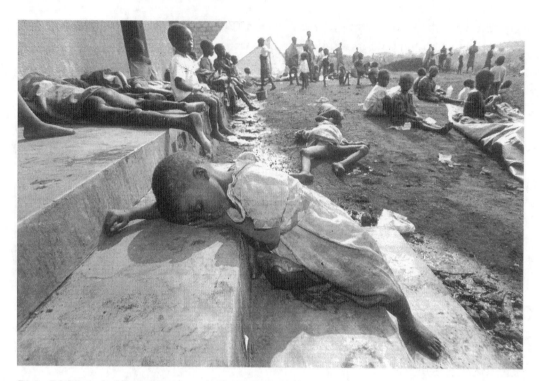

Figure 5.1 Victims of Rwandan genocide, Zaire, April 1994.
Source: Corrine Dufka, used by permission.

criminal law was developed, refined, and expanded. For example, systematic rape as a tactic of war came to be defined as a war crime.

The ad hoc tribunals were designed to be temporary and their jurisdiction was limited to crimes perpetrated only in those two regions. But they provided a model for a permanent institution with global jurisdiction. In 1998, an international meeting was convened in Rome, Italy, to draft a new treaty to establish an **International Criminal Court (ICC)**. During this process, U.S. representatives involved in treaty-drafting insisted on compromises and language that would minimize if not altogether prevent any prospect that an American might someday be put on trial at the ICC.

President Bill Clinton signed the ICC treaty in his very last hours in office, but said he was not recommending it for ratification by Congress. President George W. Bush removed the U.S. signature when he came to office. When the treaty acquired the needed number of signatures in July 2002, the ICC was established in The Hague. In August 2002, Congress passed a federal law authorizing the president to use "all means necessary and appropriate to bring about the release of any US or allied personnel being detained or imprisoned by, on behalf of, or at the request of the [ICC]." (This law was nicknamed by critics "The Hague Invasion Act.") The U.S.

government, sometimes using the carrot-and-stick of foreign aid, forced dozens of countries to sign bilateral immunity agreements pledging mutual refusal to cooperate with the ICC.

Universal Jurisdiction and the "Pinochet Precedent"

In 1998, former Chilean dictator and "Senator for Life" Augusto Pinochet traveled to London on a personal visit. At home, he had not been held accountable for the crimes perpetrated when he was in office (see Chapter 3). What happened to Pinochet during that London trip had enormous significance for the enforceability of international criminal law, and in particular for the crime of torture. A Spanish judge named Baltazar Garzón issued an international arrest warrant for Pinochet and requested the British government to extradite him to Spain to stand trial. Garzón invoked the doctrine of **universal jurisdiction** to justify this request.

Universal jurisdiction dates back to the 19th century. It was invented to make piracy and slave *trading* (not slavery itself) international crimes. Because those activities took place on the high seas, in order to put pirates and slave traders on trial anywhere, the gap in existing jurisdictional doctrines (territorial, personal, and protective) had to be closed. The rationale for *universal* jurisdiction was that piracy and slave trading were such a danger to international peace and security that every state had an interest in prosecuting perpetrators. Pirates and slave traders were classified as "enemies of all mankind" (*hostis humani generis*) who deserved no sanctuary. Through the invention of universal jurisdiction, states were given the added legal power and right to prosecute them or extradite them to another state for prosecution if petitioned to do so.

In the 20th century, the use of universal jurisdiction became an archaic remnant of the maritime world—until 1998. However, recent developments in international law, especially the work of the ad hoc tribunals for Rwanda and the former Yugoslavia, demonstrated that individuals could be punished for core crimes under international law.

Garzón and his human rights allies believed that Pinochet's crimes made him an enemy of all humankind and, therefore, Spain had an interest and a right to prosecute him. To the surprise of Pinochet and his allies, including former British prime minister Margaret Thatcher and former U.S. secretary of state Henry Kissinger (who helped orchestrate the coup that brought Pinochet to power), the British police honored the Spanish warrant and arrested Pinochet.

Through the arrest warrant, Garzón attempted to broaden the definition of genocide to include *political enemies* because thousands of people the Pinochet regime murdered were killed for political reasons rather than because of their racial, ethnical, religious, or national identity. The British Law Lords (the United Kingdom's highest judicial authorities) rejected that attempt to rewrite the law of genocide.

Moreover, they decided that *any* allegations of murder are not extraditable offenses because they occurred in the context of war—the "war on communism" raging through Latin America in the 1970s. The Law Lords maintained that killing enemies is a legitimate function of a state in war. Therefore, Pinochet enjoyed sovereign immunity from foreign prosecution for killings that occurred during this war.

However, in a landmark decision in 1999, the Law Lords ruled that torture *is* an extraditable offense for which there is no sovereign immunity because torture is not a legitimate function of any state. The "**Pinochet precedent**" held that even a former head of state could be extradited and prosecuted for torture under the doctrine of universal jurisdiction. Thus, in the final year of the 20th century, universal jurisdiction acquired a modern purpose: to prosecute people in a foreign legal system regardless of whether that country had any connection to the crime. Torture was, again, the break-out issue.

Ultimately, Pinochet was not extradited to Spain because of a political decision by British officials that he was too old and demented to stand trial. But back in Chile, his all-powerful mystique had been shattered, and he destroyed the image of being too demented by giving victory speeches to his supporters when he got home. The Chilean government stripped him of his immunity on the grounds that it violated the Chilean constitution, and made plans to put him on trial (Dorfman 2002). He avoided that fate by dying.

The Pinochet precedent invigorated and altered debates about how and where justice for torture and other core crimes could be pursued. A number of countries, mainly in Europe, created or strengthened national laws to enable the prosecution of foreigners in their courts. Since 1999, dozens of people have been prosecuted on the basis of universal jurisdiction.

Superpower Torture and Universal Jurisdiction

In 2001 and 2002, when the Bush administration was secretly devising an interrogation policy that disregarded the prohibition of torture, as I discuss in Chapter 1, the Pinochet precedent was one of the factors that officials took into consideration when they urged the president to *declare* that the Geneva Conventions do not apply to the war on terror. Their thinking was that such a declaration would immunize Americans who authorized or abetted torture from any future prospect of prosecution in a foreign national legal system. They were wrong.

A variety of efforts have been mounted in foreign countries to investigate aspects of the U.S. interrogation and detention policy and, in some countries, to criminally indict officials responsible for torture and other offenses against prisoners (see Hajjar 2010; Kaleck 2009; Ratner and Center for Constitutional Rights 2008). Here is a partial list:

- In 2004, a criminal complaint was introduced in Germany against Defense Secretary Donald Rumsfeld and a dozen civilian and military officials on behalf of Iraqi victims of torture at Abu Ghraib. Under intense U.S. diplomatic pressure, the German prosecutor dismissed the case on the principle that a foreign court cannot assert jurisdiction for a case that is being pursued in a more appropriate venue, despite the fact that there was no criminal investigation of Rumsfeld or the others named in the complaint in the United States at the time.

- In 2006, a second case was brought in Germany against Rumsfeld and several Bush administration lawyers accused of being the architects of the torture policy. This criminal complaint contained substantial new information about Rumsfeld's role in the torture of prisoners at Guantánamo. In 2007, the prosecutor dismissed the case because none of those named in the complaint was present in Germany and therefore a conviction would be unlikely.

- Following an exposé in *The Washington Post* (Priest 2005) that the CIA engaged in kidnappings and ran black sites in Europe (subsequently revealed by Human Rights Watch to be in Poland, Romania, and Lithuania), the Council of Europe conducted an investigation and in 2006 reported that approximately 100 people had been kidnapped on the continent. The European Parliament's 2007 investigative report exposed extensive collusion by European security services and other government agencies with the CIA's extraordinary rendition program. In January 2011, a Polish prosecutor conducting a criminal investigation into the CIA black site in that country recognized that Abu Zubaydah (the first "high-value detainee" taken into CIA custody in 2002) was a victim of torture. That criminal investigation is ongoing.

- In 2005, an Italian court issued indictments for 26 CIA agents (along with four Italian agents) who kidnapped Hassan Mustafa Osama Nasr (aka Abu Omar) in Milan in February 2003 and transported him to Egypt where he was brutally tortured. Despite U.S. diplomatic pressure and political opposition by the Italian government, the agents' trial-in-absentia proceeded. In November 2009, the Italian court handed down guilty verdicts for most of them. Although the Italian government refused to request the extradition of the convicted agents, the arrest warrants are active and those people would be at risk of arrest if they ever travel to a country with an extradition treaty with Italy, which includes all of Europe.

- On October 26, 2007, after Rumsfeld was out of office, efforts were made to indict him while he was in Paris. His movement was being tracked by human rights organizations and a criminal complaint had been prepared. When Rumsfeld learned of the complaint, he exited through a side door of the building where he was giving a speech in order to avoid lawyers and reporters waiting for him outside. The complaint was dismissed by the Parisian prosecutor in 2008 on

the erroneous legal reasoning that officials have immunity for activities connected to their work; there is no legal immunity for torture.

- In November 2010, George W. Bush published his memoir, *Decision Points*. In this book and in subsequent media interviews, he acknowledged (not for the first time) that he had authorized waterboarding and other "enhanced interrogation tactics" that are widely regarded as torture. In February 2011, he canceled plans to travel to Switzerland to speak at a gala benefit because a criminal complaint had been filed against him in Geneva.

- In 2007, a German court issued arrest warrants for 13 CIA agents involved in the January 2004 kidnapping of Khaled El-Masri, a German citizen, from Macedonia. El-Masri was transported to Afghanistan where he was held incommunicado for months at a black site. When the CIA agents realized that he was not who they thought he was (an al-Qaeda operative with a similar name), officials ordered his release. But instead of transporting him home to Germany, he was secretly dumped in a remote area of Albania. Eventually, he made it home. A German investigation revealed that he had been subjected to human experimentation, shot up with psychoactive drugs repeatedly over the six months of his custody. This was proven through hair, nail, and skin samples (Horton 2010). Ultimately, U.S. diplomatic pressure succeeded in squelching the case in Germany. El-Masri is suing the Macedonian government for colluding in his torture before the European Court of Human Rights.

- In May 2010, Spanish prosecutors issued indictments for the same 13 CIA agents who had kidnapped El-Masri because they had transited through Spain using false documents. Another case in Spain involves efforts to criminally investigate six Bush administration lawyers for their role in devising the torture policy and, therefore, abetting the torture of Spanish nationals and residents detained at Guantánamo. Garzón was one of the judges spearheading this investigation, which, as of this writing, remains alive despite U.S. diplomatic pressure (see Hajjar 2012).

As long as torture is recognized as a crime for which there is no legal immunity, and as long as the U.S. government refuses to criminally investigate and prosecute those officials who are responsible for torture (Human Rights Watch 2011), foreign prosecution remains a possibility.

DISCUSSION QUESTIONS

1. Based on what you have read in this and previous chapters, why do you think the U.S. government takes such a hostile position toward the ICC? Do you agree or disagree with the government's position?

2. Khaled El-Masri is one of many innocent people who were tortured by U.S. agents. What, in your opinion, would "justice" for El-Masri look like?
3. If a former U.S. official was arrested and put on trial for torture in a foreign country, and you were asked to write an opinion piece for a local newspaper, what would you say?

VI: What's Wrong with Torture?

Torture is not only illegal and immoral. It is damaging and destructive. Obviously, torture damages victims—hurting people on purpose is the very definition of this practice. But it also damages torturers, and perpetrating institutions, and even in some contexts whole societies. In this final chapter, I offer some facts and insights about the negative effects of torture.

Torture from the Perspective of Victims

Jean Améry, a Belgian Jew, who was tortured by the Nazis before being sent to a concentration camp, survived and wrote about his ordeals. "[O]n the basis of an experience that in no way probed the entire range of possibilities, I dare to assert that torture is the most horrible event a human being can retain within himself" (1980: 22). He describes how torture affected him: "The first blow brings home to the prisoner that he is *helpless*" and he loses "trust in the world" (pp. 27, 28). If Améry's torturers were motivated to produce these subjective experiences, then from his perspective, it worked very well. "Whoever was tortured, stays tortured" (p. 34). However, if the purpose was to obtain information important to the Nazi war effort, torture made him speak, but he had nothing of value to say: "I accused myself of invented absurd political crimes … Apparently I had the hope that, after such incriminating disclosures, a well-aimed blow to the head would put an end to my misery" (p. 36).

The pain and suffering of torture may stop, but the experience is permanent, indelible. Because torture usually takes place in clandestine settings, much of what is known comes from victims. Some victims' experiences are documented in human rights reports or described by journalists and scholars (Conroy 2000; Danner 2009a, 2009b; Harbury 2005; Worthington 2007). Some, like Améry, recount them in autobiographies (see Kurnaz 2008; Ortiz 2002; Timerman 1981).

Victims' torture experience or their after-effects are the topic of many novels, poems, and movies. Ariel Dorfman's play *Death and the Maiden* (1990) is a fictionalized account of real torture in his native country, Chile. The story, which begins after the end of military rule, exposes the difficulty of *getting past the past* in a society where many people were tortured. The central character, Paulina, is a torture survivor. Most of the story takes place over one long night, which begins when her husband comes home with a Good Samaritan who gave him a ride after he got a flat tire. Paulina is convinced that this man is the doctor who repeatedly raped her in prison. Her husband did not know—until that night—that she had been raped; she had kept that fact a secret from him. I won't spoil the ending by telling you what happens, but suffice it to say that Paulina would agree with Améry that whoever was tortured stays tortured. *Death and the Maiden* was made into a movie directed by Roman Polanski (1994).

By many victims' accounts, sexualized torture is the worst experience. Rape, sexual mutilation, forced nakedness, and humiliation are used to exploit individuals' most susceptible physical and psychological vulnerabilities, to degrade and dehumanize them, and to destroy their relations with families and communities (see Thornhill 1992). Public awareness of sexual torture as a tactic of warfare increased following the conflict in the former Yugoslavia (see Chapter 5). A documentary, *Calling the Ghosts* (Jacobson and Jelincic 1996), features two Bosnian Muslim female lawyers who survived the Serbian concentration camp of Omarska. The film traces how they came to terms with their own rapes and then worked to document the abuses that they and their fellow female prisoners suffered. When the UN established an ad hoc tribunal, their experiences and documentation were instrumental in preparing indictments for perpetrators from Omarska. The work of that tribunal led to the reform of international law to make rape a war crime.

The sexual torture of males is underreported because survivors often internalize gender stereotypes of men as aggressors and women as victims, as well as the social stigma of same-sex contact. In 2004 in Egypt, dozens of men suspected of homosexual activity (which is a criminal offense in that country) were arrested and sexually tortured to elicit confessions of their allegedly transgressive behavior and to shame and humiliate them (Human Rights Watch 2004). Mustafa Dirani, a Lebanese militia leader who was kidnapped in 1994 by the Israeli military and detained in a secret prison for six years, brought a lawsuit against the Israeli government. (His lawyer was a former Israeli intelligence agent.) At Dirani's hearing in Tel Aviv on January 27, 2004, he testified that he was raped by one soldier and sodomized by the head of the interrogation team (Menicucci 2005: 18).

The photographing of naked prisoners serves as a *shame multiplier* by compounding the dehumanizing experience. Moazzem Begg, a British citizen arrested in Pakistan in 2001 and shipped to Afghanistan where he spent a year in U.S. custody before being transferred to Guantánamo, described his arrival at the U.S. prison in Kandahar: After being thrown, shackled to the ground and mounted by several soldiers, "I felt a cold, sharp metal object against my legs: they were using a knife to slice off all my clothes … I was pulled up to a standing position and the hood was removed … I was confronted with the sight of soldiers encircling me, screaming abuse and taking pictures again" (Begg with Brittain 2006: 111).

The only novel aspect of the sexualized humiliation and torture that occurred in the Abu Ghraib prison in Iraq was the abundance and publication of photos of naked

Figure 6.1 Prisoner abuse at Abu Ghraib.
Source: The Abu Ghraib Files.

prisoners being forced to masturbate and mounted in pyramids by U.S. soldiers. An Iraqi man in one of the naked pyramids that people around the world have seen later gave sworn testimony that he would have killed himself that night if he had had the means (Danner 2004: 240). One of the women victims of torture and rape at Abu Ghraib sent a letter begging insurgents to bomb the prison and kill everyone inside—including herself—so the suffering could end (Apel 2005: 99). There are more—allegedly much worse—pictures and videos of rape and torture at Abu Ghraib that the public has never seen because they remain classified.

The political context can affect how victims experience being tortured. When torture is used in the context of war or conflict, sometimes those who are fighting for a cause for which they are prepared to sacrifice regard their interrogation as a form of "battle." In his ethnographic study, *Formations of Violence*, Allen Feldman (1991) locates Britain's use of the five techniques on Irish Republican Army (IRA) prisoners within the broader conflict for Irish independence (see Chapter 3). Feldman's informants, at least the more hardened paramilitaries ("hard men"), discussed interrogation as part of a national struggle in which they were actively engaged. Some of them asserted power through "counter-instrumentation" of their own bodies, for example, provoking a beating to force the interrogator to play his ace card right away, thereby diminishing his control (see also Doumani 1996).

The Effects of Torture on Perpetrators

In comparison to victim-focused literature and victims' testimonials, accounts by and scholarship about perpetrators of torture are more limited. Most first-hand accounts come from ex-torturers or others who worked in interrogation sites (Crelinsten 1993; Neely 2008; Saar and Novak 2005; Sharrock 2008). Information also comes from testimonies at court martial or other kinds of prosecutorial proceedings, and from truth and reconciliation processes in post-conflict societies. Documentaries about U.S. torture that feature first-person accounts by Americans who perpetrated or witnessed prisoner abuse include *Taxi to the Dark Side* (Gibney 2007), *Ghosts of Abu Ghraib* (Kennedy 2007), and *Standard Operating Procedure* (Morris 2008).

Huggins, Hariras - Falousos, and Zimbardo's (2002) *Violence Workers*, which focuses on Brazilian police during the military regime, provides an interdisciplinary analysis about why ordinary men torture for the state and how they explain and justify their violence. The authors find that four interrelated patterns structure their experiences: *(a)* secrecy of their mission, *(b)* the insularity and isolation of torture units, *(c)* a division of violent labor, and *(d)* personal isolation and social separation in their daily lives (p. 2). In Brazil, as in many other contexts, torturers' self-perceptions of their activities and roles were shaped by the prevailing national security ideology, the dehumanization of enemies, and norms of obedience within military institutions. Mark Osiel's (2004) research on the mental state of Argentine torturers highlights the influential role of Catholic clergy in persuading soldiers to overcome the "moral enormity" of torturing and killing prisoners by framing these activities in just war and biblical terms, for example citing the parable of separating wheat from chaff.

Wartime interrogators, especially those engaged in unconventional wars between states and non-state groups, are encouraged and likely to regard their work as a kind of frontline service because actionable intelligence is ammunition against elusive or civilian enemies. According to Chris Mackey (pseudonym), one of the first U.S. military interrogators sent to the Afghan war zone in 2001, pressure was intense for actionable intelligence—especially the whereabouts of Osama bin Laden and other top al-Qaeda and Taliban leaders. The message from the Pentagon moving down the chain of command was that detainees were guilty fonts of valuable information, and that their claims of innocence or ignorance were signs of their deceptive skillfulness. "Strictly speaking, that meant every Arab we encountered was in for a long-term stay and an eventual trip to Cuba" (Mackey and Miller 2004: 85). However, as Mackey explains, "They were bringing back a lot of fighters. But they were also bringing back a lot of farmers" (p. 115).

In contexts where interrogation rules are muddled or unenforced, interrogators might develop torturous innovations (Ron 1997; Soufan 2011). By December 2001, Pentagon officials were exploring how to "reverse engineer" SERE (survival, evasion, resistance, extraction) techniques that had been developed during the Cold War to train U.S. soldiers to withstand torture in case they were captured by regimes that don't adhere to the Geneva Conventions. The kinds of "counter-resistance" techniques that became standard operating procedure for military interrogators included protracted hooding, sleep deprivation, recurrent body cavity searches, chaining and tying detainees to chairs or hooks on the floor or wall, forcible shaving, and death threats.

As in any kind of specialized work, torturers must learn to master their craft (Rejali 2007: 420–25, 573–79). Military training to endure pain and suffering can be used to overcome individuals' natural aversion to inflicting pain and suffering on others (Crelinsten 1993: 56; Mayer 2005), and witnessing or assisting in torture can provide the social situational pressures to comply and conform.

The power that torturers have over prisoners can foster negative transformations in some perpetrators' personalities (Haney 2000; Zimbardo 2007). This might include a dangerous expansion of ego, escalating cruelty, and lasting emotional disorders (McCoy 2006: 9; Rejali 2007: 524–26). While such experiences are not universal, there are no studies objectively attesting that torture is a positive and enriching experience for perpetrators.

Torture can have pathological effects on perpetrating institutions and on the societies in which they operate. Brazilian torturers turned into smugglers, blackmailers, and extortionists and eventually were purged from the army "to save the army" (McCoy 2006: 77). The Philippines during the dictatorship of Ferdinand Marcos provides a potent lesson about the corrosive effects of torture on the nation's military. Rogue units, who got their start as torturers, mounted more coup attempts in the eighties than in any other country at that time, and through the early nineties they waged a protracted civil war and perpetrated numerous acts of domestic terrorism.

The practice of torture is embedded in larger institutional settings within prisons and interrogation centers. According to research on torture survivors, between one-third and one-half report that physicians were present during—in some cases overseeing—their abuse (Miles 2006). Information that American doctors and psychologists were involved in prisoner abuse first emerged in 2004 when an International Committee of the Red Cross report characterizing Guantánamo tactics as "tantamount to torture" was leaked to the press (Bloche and Marks 2005). The involvement of psychologists in devising and implementing abusive interrogation procedures spurred a protracted dispute within the American Psychological Association (Soldz and Olson 2008).

Does Torture Work? Lessons from the U.S. Case

Tens of thousands of people were arrested and detained by the United States in the war on terror. Many were innocent or had no meaningful intelligence. Some were swept up in raids, sold to the United States for bounty, named by others under torture, or victims of mistaken identities. But many of them remained in custody and continued to be abusively interrogated long after their innocence or intelligence valuelessness was known to officials (see Danner 2009b).

A vast amount of information about the U.S. interrogation and detention policy has become public over the last decade. This includes thousands of pages of policy documents and memoranda, and unclassified reports of official investigations (see www.thetorturedatabase.org). Although many details and documents remain classified, enough information has come to light to draw some conclusions about an important question: "Does torture work?"

Indeed, the torture debate has evolved into a dispute about whether *American torture* worked *for America*. Pro-torture consequentialists (see Chapter 1) believe that torture can make—and claim that it has made—prisoners say true and useful things. Others, including experts in interrogation (Swenson 2006), rebut the contention that pain, suffering, and humiliation are effective means of eliciting truth, a problem that is compounded when interrogators do not know the answers to their questions and thus cannot judge whether what people they are torturing say is true (Arrigo 2003; Scheppele 2005; Soufan 2011). Those who engage the question from a broader perspective consider how the practice of torture has served or harmed the goals and objectives that motivated its authorization and justified its use (e.g. military victory, enhancement of national security).

In the spring of 2009, the American torture debate crescendoed when three high-profile interlocutors took to the public stage. Former Vice President Cheney and former FBI agent Ali Soufan represented, respectively, the pro- and anti-torture positions, and President Barack Obama addressed the broader perspective on torture's effects.

In a May 21 speech at the American Enterprise Institute, Cheney insisted that "our enhanced interrogation program ... [was] used on hardened terrorists after other efforts failed ... [The use of these methods] prevented the violent death of thousands, if not hundreds of thousands, of innocent people." Cheney claimed the existence of classified documents that prove that CIA interrogations produced valuable intelligence. He said, "Over on the left wing of the president's party, there appears to be little curiosity in finding out what was learned from the terrorists." On May 29, Carl Levin, chair of the Senate Armed Services Committee, reported that he had examined the documents to which Cheney was referring, which "say nothing about numbers of lives saved, nor do the documents connect acquisition of valuable intelligence to the use of abusive techniques. I hope that the documents are declassified, so that people can judge for themselves what is fact, and what is fiction." (For a debunking of claims that disaster-averting actionable intelligence was elicited through torture, see Horton 2009; Luban 2008; Rose 2008; Suskind 2006.)

Soufan, an Arabic-speaking top al-Qaeda profiler, interrogated Abu Zubaydah, the first high-value detainee (HVD), when he was captured in early 2002. In an April 2009 op-ed in *The New York Times*, Soufan broke his seven-year silence about "the false claims magnifying the effectiveness of the so-called enhanced interrogation techniques." On May 13, he testified at a Senate Judiciary Committee hearing that he had used conventional (not torture) interrogation methods of deception and rapport-building, which succeeded in getting Abu Zubaydah to talk, including revealing the identity of the 9/11 "mastermind," Khalid Sheikh Muhammad (KSM). At that point, a CIA team headed by a psychologist contractor with no interrogation experience took over. They stripped Abu Zubaydah naked and began using harsh tactics. He stopped talking. Several days later, Soufan and his team were permitted to resume their interrogation, but when he started talking, the CIA took over again, and again he stopped talking. The third time the CIA took over, Soufan got so agitated at the illegal and ineffective methods they were using that he called FBI headquarters and threatened to arrest the CIA agents on the spot. His team was pulled out, and the FBI stopped cooperating with the CIA on interrogations. Soufan's (2011) autobiography, *The Black Banners*, is an authoritative refutation of Cheney's claim that harsh methods were used as a *last resort* after other methods had failed.

The truth about Abu Zubaydah's treatment is important because it set the stage for the CIA interrogation program. As I note in Chapter 1, his importance had been overestimated. Contrary to claims that he was al-Qaeda's chief of operations, in fact, he was the "emir" of one of the training camps for Islamist Militants (Mujahideen) in Afghanistan and wasn't even a member of al-Qaeda on 9/11. Over the years he was held in black sites, Abu Zubayda talked. But he did not have the kinds of actionable intelligence he was erroneously assumed to possess. According to former officials who followed his interrogations, "not a single significant plot was foiled as a result of [his] tortured confessions." Rather, he made false statements about planned attacks on shopping malls, nuclear plants, the Brooklyn Bridge, and the Statue of Liberty that "sent hundreds of CIA and FBI investigators scurrying in pursuit of phantoms" (Finn and Warrick 2009). Think about what that tells us about the hypothetical ticking bomb scenario.

Unlike most prisoners detained by the United States, KSM *was* a valuable intelligence asset. He was captured in 2003 when someone turned him in for a $25 million reward. KSM was waterboarded 183 times and subjected to the panoply of tactics in the CIA's repertoire. According to former CIA and Pentagon officials with direct knowledge of his interrogations, most of what he said under torture was lies, and he gave up no actionable intelligence. According to David Rose (2008), who interviewed numerous counter-terrorist officials, their conclusions were unanimous: "[N]ot only have coercive methods failed to generate significant and actionable intelligence, they have also caused the squandering of resources on a massive scale …, chimerical plots, and unnecessary safety alerts." Thus, the indirect costs of U.S. torture include the misallocation of resources to follow false leads.

The other key pro-torture claim that the use of harsh methods was motivated by the need to prevent future attacks has become far less plausible in light of information in declassified documents. The Bush administration's desire to justify expanding the war on terror to Iraq caused a major spike in the weeks prior to the 2003 invasion.

CIA and military interrogators were under intense pressure to produce evidence that would persuade the American public and allied governments that Iraq was actively engaged in developing weapons of mass destruction (WMD) and that the regime of Saddam Hussein had links to al-Qaeda (Horton 2009). The evidence that the administration presented to make the case for war included the claim that Iraq had trained al-Qaeda operatives in the use of chemical weapons. This was extracted by torture from a Libyan prisoner, Ibn al-Shaykh al-Libi, who was extraordinarily rendered by the CIA to Egypt. Al-Libi had lied to his interrogators to make the pain stop. A second spike occurred several months into the occupation of Iraq, and was motivated to stay cracks in public support for the war because the (nonexistent) WMD failed to materialize and an anti-U.S. insurgency was raising the American death toll. The Abu Ghraib debacle was the product of a desperate quest for intelligence because the Bush administration was suffering politically at home.

The third interlocutor, President Obama, offered a broader perspective on the effects of torture. On a March 22, 2009 segment on *60 Minutes*, he said, "I fundamentally disagree with Dick Cheney." He elaborated on this disagreement in a May 21 speech to the nation in which he said,

> [Brutal methods] undermine the rule of law. They alienate us in the world. They serve as a recruitment tool for terrorists, and increase the will of our enemies to fight us, while decreasing the will of others to work with America. They risk the lives of our troops by making it less likely that others will surrender to them in battle, and more likely that Americans will be mistreated if they are captured. In short, they did not advance our war and counter-terrorism efforts—they undermined them.

One of the themes of Obama's May 21 speech was how the use of torture has fouled prospects for bringing the perpetrators of 9/11 to justice. He described the situation he had inherited as a "legal mess." The Bush administration had attempted to circumvent the problem of prosecuting people who had been tortured by establishing rules for the military commissions that would admit coerced evidence. Six military prosecutors quit rather than going along with such a system (Horton 2008a; Umansky 2008). In November 2008, the convening authority (top official) for the military commissions ruled that Muhammad al-Qahtani, the prisoner suspected of being the 20th hijacker—and for whom the "special measures" at Guantánamo were initially devised (Sands 2008)—was not prosecutable *because* he had been tortured.

Only three people, none of them charged with planning 9/11 or being terrorist leaders, were prosecuted in the military commissions during the Bush years. A few more have been prosecuted during the Obama years. KSM and four other detainees accused of perpetrating 9/11 have been charged for trial. But their torture at the hands of the CIA is making this extremely difficult *for the government*, and experts estimate that their trial will take years.

How American Torture Hurts Americans

The torture policy has had deadly consequences for U.S. forces as well as civilians in Iraq, Afghanistan, and elsewhere. The torture of Arabs and Muslims has been a major recruitment tool for al-Qaeda and other terrorist organizations (Alexander and Bruning 2008; Herrington 2007). According to Matthew Alexander (pseudonym), a retired Air Force major with extensive interrogation experience in Iraq, the primary reason foreign fighters gave for coming to Iraq was the torture and abuse at Abu Ghraib and Guantánamo. In an interview he stated:

> Because the majority of US casualties and injuries are the result of suicide bombings, most which are carried out by foreign fighters, at least hundreds but more likely thousands of American lives (not to count Iraqi civilian deaths) are linked directly to the policy decision to introduce the torture and abuse of prisoners as accepted tactics.
>
> (Horton 2008b)

Former top Navy lawyer Alberto Mora testified to the Senate Armed Services Committee in 2008 that "there are serving US flag-rank officers who maintain that the first and second identifiable causes of US combat deaths in Iraq … are, respectively, the symbols of Abu Ghraib and Guantánamo."

To date, no one has studied whether there is a direct connection between post-traumatic stress disorder (PTSD) and the perpetration or witnessing of torture by U.S. soldiers and contractors, although this connection is the subject of Joshua Phillips' (2010) *None of Us Were Like This Before: American Soldiers and Torture*. (For a study of atrocity perpetration and PTSD drawn from earlier conflicts, see MacNair 2002.) PTSD afflicts American veterans at epidemic rates, with tragic consequences that include suicides (currently at a rate of more than one per day), as well as drug and alcohol abuse, domestic violence, and other violent crimes (Leopold 2011). The PTSD-causing effects of fearing, witnessing, or surviving suicide bombing attacks and the causal connection between these attacks and the torture policy (as Alexander and Mora state) suggest at least an indirect causal connection. Moreover, this PTSD epidemic among soldiers and veterans adversely affects the entire military, as well as families, communities, and indeed American society as a whole. These costs should be part of the calculation in determining whether torture is effective and necessary.

Conclusion

The legacy of American torture confirms timeless truisms about the dubious relationship between pain and truth. "Torture," as 3rd-century AD/CE Roman jurist Ulpian observed, "is a difficult and deceptive thing[,] for the strong will resist and the weak will say anything to end the pain." As for truth, according to the German Jesuit Friedrich von Spee in 1631, "It is incredible what people say under the compulsion of torture, and how many lies they will tell about themselves and about others; in the end, whatever the torturers want to be true, is true." For a contemporary judgment, Darius Rejali (2007: 478) explains the ineffectiveness and destructiveness of torture, which fits the U.S. case: "[O]rganized torture yields poor information, sweeps up many innocents, degrades organizational capabilities, and destroys interrogators. Limited time during battle or emergency intensifies all these problems."

There is substantial evidence that policy decisions to harm and humiliate prisoners did not produce "excellent" intelligence, and these policies certainly did not win the war on terror. Rather, it generated a vast amount of false and useless information, and efforts to investigate that information wasted valuable time and resources. This evidence should silence assertions that such methods are a necessary "lesser evil." Rejali writes, "Apologists often assume that torture works … [but if it] does not work, then their apology is irrelevant" (2007: 447).

Lessons from the U.S. case confirm that torture cannot be employed with strategic precision; the anti-torture deontologists (see Chapter 1) were right: there is no such thing as just a little torture.

What the Uniated States lacked and desperately needed after 9/11 was human intelligence about al-Qaeda and affiliated organizations. But the decision to "take the gloves off" to compensate for the lack of intelligence had the reverse effects: It undermined the willingness of critical constituencies to cooperate, notably those in which terrorist organizations operate and populations to whom they appeal for support. By indiscriminately arresting so many people and by subjecting so many to violent and dehumanizing treatment, the quest for assistance in those communities, let alone hearts and minds, was damned. Torture squandered the "we are all Americans" global empathy after 9/11 and invited righteous condemnation by informed citizens and allied foreign governments.

Perhaps the most important lesson is the falseness of the trade-off theory that human rights must be sacrificed for security when contending with the threat of terrorism. Pro-torture consequentialists argue that respect for the legal rights of suspects constrains the government's options to protect the nation. However, a recent study by Walsh and Piazza (2009) finds that government respect for "physical integrity rights" (i.e. the "harder human rights" as discussed in Chapter 4) is consistently and significantly associated with *fewer* terrorist attacks. Respect for these rights, of which the right not to be tortured is supremely important, are so critical because their violation is so universally offensive. As Walsh and Piazza argue, respecting physical integrity rights by not torturing (or extra-judicially executing) suspects is more effective because it legitimizes counter-terror efforts and fosters active or passive support from crucial constituencies. Conversely, violations of the right not to be tortured confirm or increase the grievances that motivate people to oppose a government.

At a very high cost to victims, perpetrators, and society, the U.S. case illustrates that no modern regime or society is *more* secure as a result of torture. On the contrary, its use spreads, its harms multiply, and its corrosive consequences boost rather than diminish the threats of terrorism and the number of people who count themselves as enemies.

Keeping torture illegal and struggling to enforce the right not to be tortured are the front lines, quite literally, of a global battle to defend the most universal right that all human beings can claim. If torture is legitimized and legalized in the future, it is not "the terrorists" who will lose but "the humans." Should proponents of torture as a "lesser evil" succeed in regaining legitimacy for this odious practice, there would be no better words than George Orwell's from *1984*: "If you want a picture of the future, imagine a boot stamping on a human face—forever."

DISCUSSION QUESTIONS

1. As you recall, in Chapter 1, I asked whether you think torture might be legitimate "sometimes" or "often." How did you answer then, and how—if at all—has your answer changed?
2. The motivation of U.S. officials to authorize torture was the legitimate need to "keep Americans safe." Based on what you have read, do you feel safer as a result of torture?
3. If you were invited to the White House to discuss the war on terror and the legacy of the torture policy, what message would you convey to the president?

References

N.B.: All web material accessed May 30, 2012.

Abrahamian, Ervand. 1999. *Tortured Confessions: Prisons and Public Recantations in Modern Iran.* Berkeley: University of California Press.

Alexander, Matthew, and John Bruning. 2008. *How to Break a Terrorist: The US Interrogators Who Used Brains, Not Brutality, To Take Down the Deadliest Man in Iraq.* New York: Free Press.

Alleg, Henri. 2006. *The Question.* Translation J. Calder. Lincoln, NE: Bison Books.

Altman, Robert. 1970. *M.A.S.H.* (movie). Los Angeles: Twentieth Century Fox.

Améry Jean. 1980. *At the Mind's Limits: Contemplations by a Survivor on Auschwitz and Its Realities.* Translation S. Rosenfeld and S. P. Rosenfeld. Bloomington: Indiana University Press.

Amnesty International. 2002. *USA: Treatment of Prisoners in Afghanistan and Guantánamo Bay Undermines Human Rights.*

Apel, Dora. 2005. "Torture Culture: Lynching Photographs and the Images of Abu Ghraib." *Art Journal 64*: 88–100.

Arendt, Hannah. 1973. *The Origins of Totalitarianism.* New York: A Harvest Book.

Arrigo, Jean. 2003. "A Consequentialist Argument against Torture Interrogation of Terrorists." Presented at Joint Services Conference on Professional Ethics, January. 30–31, Springfield, VA. http://www.au.af.mil/au/awc/awcgate/jscope/arrigo03.htm

Aussaresses, Paul. 2002. *The Battle of the Casbah: Terrorism and Counter-Terrorism in Algeria, 1955–1957.* New York: Enigma Books.

Begg, Moazzam, with Victoria Brittain. 2006. *Enemy Combatant: A British Muslim's Journey to Guantánamo and Back.* New York: Free Press.

Bernstein, Richard. 2009. "At Last, Justice for Monsters." *New York Review of Books 56* (April 9). http://www.nybooks.com/articles/archives/2009/apr/09/at-last-justice-for-monsters/?pagination=false.

Bloche, M. Gregg, and Jonathan H. Marks. 2005. "Doctors and Interrogators at Guantánamo Bay." *New England Journal of Medicine 353*: 6–8.

Bowden, Mark. 2003. "The Dark Art of Interrogation." *Atlantic Monthly 292* (October): 51–58, 60, 62, 64–65, 68–70, 72–74, 76.

Bumiller, Kristen. 1988. *The Civil Rights Society: The Social Construction of Victims.* Baltimore: Johns Hopkins University Press.

Bush, George W. 2010. *Decision Points.* New York: Crown.

Butler, Judith. 2004. *Precarious Life: The Powers of Mourning and Violence.* New York: Verso.

Chandler, David. 2000. *Voices from S-21: Terror and History in Pol Pot's Secret Prison*. Berkeley: University of California Press.

Cohen, Stanley. 2001. *States of Denial: Knowing about Atrocities and Suffering*. Cambridge, UK: Polity.

Conroy, John. 2000. *Unspeakable Acts, Ordinary People: The Dynamics of Torture*. Berkeley: University of California Press.

Crelinsten, Ronald D. 1993. "In Their Own Words: The World of the Torturer." *The Politics of Pain: Torturers and Their Masters*, eds. R. D. Crelinsten and A. P. Schmid, Pp. 39–72. Leiden: COMT.

Crenshaw, Kimberle. 1995. "Race, Reform and Retrenchment: Transformation and Legitimation in Anti-Discrimination Law." *Critical Race Theory*, eds. K. Crenshaw, N. Gotanda, G. Peller, and K. Thomas Pp. 103–22. New York: New Press.

Crenshaw, Kimberle, Neil Gotanda, Gary Peller, and Kendall Thomas, eds. 1995. *Critical Race Theory: The Key Writings That Formed the Movement*. New York: New Press.

Danner, Mark. 2004. *Torture and Truth: America, Abu Ghraib and the War on Terror*. New York: New York Review of Books.

——. 2009a. "US Torture: Voices from the Black Sites." *New York Review of Books 56(6)* (April. 9). http://www.nybooks.com/articles/22530.

——. 2009b. "The Red Cross Torture Report: What It Means." *New York Review of Books 56(7)* (April 30). http://www.nybooks.com/articles/22614.

Dayan, Colin. 2007. *The Story of Cruel and Unusual*. Boston: Boston Review Press.

Dershowitz, Allen. 2002a. *Shouting Fire: Civil Liberties in a Turbulent Age*. New York: Little, Brown.

——. 2002b. "Let America Take Its Cues from Israel Regarding Torture." *Jewish World Review* (January 30). http://www.jewishworldreview.com/0102/torture.asp.

——. 2003. *Why Terrorism Works: Understanding the Threat, Responding to the Challenge*. New Haven, CT: Yale University Press.

——. 2004. "Tortured Reasoning." *Torture: A Collection*, ed. Sanford Levinson, Pp. 257–80. New York: Oxford University Press.

Dorfman, Ariel. 1990. *Death and the Maiden*. New York: Penguin Books.

——. 2002. *Exorcising Terror: The Incredible Unending Trial of General Augusto Pinochet*. New York: Seven Stories Press.

Doumani, Beshara. 1996. "Israeli Interrogation Methods: A View from Jalameh: Interview with Bashar Tarabieh." *Middle East Report 201*: 29–30.

DuBois, Paige. 1991. *Torture and Truth*. New York: Routledge.

Elkins, Caroline. 2005. *Imperial Reckoning: The Untold Story of Britain's Gulag in Kenya*. New York: Owl Books.

Fanon, Frantz. 2004. *The Wretched of the Earth*. Translation R. Philcox. New York: Grove.

Feitlowitz, Marguerite. 1998. *A Lexicon of Terror: Argentina and the Legacies of Torture*. New York: Oxford University Press.

Feldman, Allen. 1991. *Formations of Violence: The Narrative of the Body and Political Terror in Northern Ireland*. Chicago: University of Chicago Press.

Finn, Peter, and Joby Warrick. 2009. "Detainee's Harsh Treatment Foiled No Plots." *Washington Post* March 29: A1.

Forrest, Duncan, ed. 1996. *A Glimpse of Hell: Reports on Torture Worldwide.* New York: New York University Press and Amnesty International.

Foucault, Michel. 1977. *Discipline and Punish: The Birth of the Prison.* Translation A. Sheridan. New York: Vintage Books.

———. 1990. *History of Sexuality, Vol. 1.* New York: Vintage.

Frankenheimer, John. 1962. *The Manchurian Candidate* (film). New York: M.C. Productions.

Galanter, Mark. 1974. "Why the 'Haves' Come Out Ahead: Speculations on the Limits of Legal Change." *Law and Society Review 9*: 95–160.

Garland, David. 1990. *Punishment and Modern Society: A Study in Sociological Theory.* Chicago: University of Chicago Press.

Gibney, Alex. 2007. *Taxi to the Dark Side* (film). New York: Velocity/ThinkFilm.

Gordon, Robert W. 1998. "Some Critical Theories of Law and Their Critics." *The Politics of Law: A Progressive Critique*, 3rd edition, ed. David Kairys, Pp. 641–66 in. New York: Basic Books.

Greenberg, Karen J. 2009. *The Least Worst Place: Guantánamo's First 100 Days.* New York: Oxford University Press.

———., ed. 2005. *The Torture Debate in America.* New York: Cambridge University Press.

Greenberg, Karen J., and Josh L. Dratel, eds. 2005. *The Torture Papers: The Road to Abu Ghraib.* New York: Cambridge University Press.

Gronke, Paul, Darius Rejali, Dustin Drenguis, James Hicks, Peter Miller, and Bryan Nakayama. 2010. "US Public Opinion on Torture, 2001–2009." *PS: Political Science and Politics 43*: 437–44.

Hagan, John, Heather Schoenfeld, and Alberto Pallone. 2006. "The Science of Human Rights, War Crimes, and Humanitarian Emergencies." *Annual Review of Sociology 32*: 329–49.

Hajjar, Lisa. 2005. *Courting Conflict: The Israeli Military Court System in the West Bank and Gaza.* Berkeley: University of California Press.

———. 2010. "Universal Jurisdiction as Praxis: An Option To Pursue Legal Accountability for Superpower Torturers." *When Governments Break the Law: The Rule of Law and the Prosecution of the Bush Administration,* eds. Austin Sarat and Nasser Hussain, Pp. 87–120 in. New York: New York University Press.

———. 2012. "Wikileaking the Truth about American Unaccountability for Torture." *Societies without Borders 7*(2): 192–225.

Haney, Craig. 2000. "Reflections on the Stanford Prison Experiment: Genesis, Transformations, Consequences." *Obedience to Authority: Current Perspectives on the Milgram Paradigm*, ed. T. Blass, Pp. 193–237 in. Mahwah, NJ: Lawrence Erlbaum.

Hansen, Suzy. 2002. "Why Terrorism Works." *Salon.com*, (September 12). http://www.salon.com/2002/09/12/dershowitz_3.

Harbury, Jennifer. 2005. *Truth, Torture and the American Way: The History and Consequences of US Involvement in Torture.* Boston: Beacon Press.

Herrington, Stuart. 2007. "Two Problems with Torture: It's Wrong and It Doesn't Work." *Pittsburgh Post-Gazette* ('October 21'). http://www.post-gazette.com/pg/07294/826876-35.stm.

Hersh, Seymour M. 2004. "Torture at Abu Ghraib: American Soldiers Brutalized Iraqis. How Far Up Does Responsibility Go?" *New Yorker*, (May 10). http://www.newyorker.com/archive/2004/05/10/040510fa_fact.

Hochschild, Alex. 1999. *King Leopold's Ghost: A Story of Greed, Terror and Heroism in Colonial Africa*. Boston: Mariner Books.

Horne, Alistair. 1978. *A Savage War of Peace: Algeria 1954–1962*. New York: Viking Books.

Horton, Scott. 2007. "State of Exception: Bush's War on the Rule of Law." *Harper's Magazine*, (July): 74–81.

——. 2008a. "Justice after Bush: Prosecuting an Outlaw Administration." *Harper's Magazine* (December): 49–60.

——. 2008b. "'The American Public Has a Right to Know that They Do Not Have to Choose between Torture and Terror': Six Questions for Matthew Alexander, author of *How To Break a Terrorist*." *Harper's Magazine*, (December 18). http://www.harpers.org/archive/2008/12/hbc-90004036.

——. 2009. "Busting the Torture Myths." *Daily Beast*, (April 27). http://www.thedailybeast.com/blogs-andstories/2009-04-27/myth-and-reality-about-torture/full.

——. 2010. "The El-Masri Cable." *Harper's Magazine*, (November 29). http://www.harpers.org/archive/2010/11/hbc-90007831.

Huggins, Martha K., Mika Haritos-Fatouros, and Philip G. Zimbardo. 2002. *Violence Workers: Police Tortures and Murders Reconstruct Brazilian Atrocities*. Berkeley: University of California Press.

Human Rights First. 2007. *Primetime Torture: Ticking Bombs, Torture and TV*. http://www.human-rightsfirst.org/us law/etn/primetime.

Human Rights Watch. 2003. *U.S.: Guantánamo Kids at Risk*. (April 23). http://www.hrw.org/en/news/2003/04/23/us-Guantánamo-kids-risk.

——. 2004. *In a Time of Torture: The Assault on Justice in Egypt's Crackdown on Homosexual Conduct*. http://www.hrw.org/en/node/12167.

——. 2011. *Getting Away with Torture: The Bush Administration and the Mistreatment of Detainees*. http://www.hrw.org/sites/default/files/reports/us0711webwcover.pdf.

Hunt, Lynn. 2007. *Inventing Human Rights: A History*. New York: Norton.

Jacobson, Mandy, and Karmen Jelincic. 1996. *Calling the Ghosts: A Story about Rape, War, and Women* (film). New York: Bowery Production.

Jaffer, Jameel, and Amrit Singh, eds. 2007. *Administration of Torture: From Washington to Abu Ghraib and Beyond*. New York: Columbia University Press.

Kaleck, Wolfgang. 2009. "From Pinochet to Rumsfeld: Universal Jurisdiction in Europe 1998–2008." *Michigan Journal of International Law 30*: 932–58.

Kennedy, Rory. 2007. *Ghosts of Abu Ghraib* (film). New York: HBO.

Khalili, Laleh. 2012. *Time in the Shadows: Confinement in Counterinsurgencies*. Palo Alto, CA: Stanford University Press.

Klein, Naomi. 2007. *The Shock Doctrine: The Rise of Disaster Capitalism*. New York: Metropolitan Books.

Kornbluh, Peter. 2003. *The Pinochet File: A Declassified Dossier on Atrocity and Accountability*. New York: New Press.

Kramer, Peter. 2008. "The Water Cure: Debating Torture and Counterinsurgency—A Century Ago." *New Yorker*, (Feburary 25). http://www.newyorker.com/reporting/2008/02/25/080225fa_fact_Kramer.

Kull, Steven, Clay Ramsay, Stephen Weber, Evan Lewis, Melinda Brouwer, Melanie Ciolek, and Abe Medoff. 2008. *World Public Opinion on Torture*. Washington, DC: World Public Opinion,

Program in International Policy Attitudes. http://www.worldpublicopinion.org/pipa/pdf/jun08/WPO_Torture_Jun08_packet.pdf.

Kurnaz, Murat. 2008. *Five Years of My Life: An Innocent Man in Guantánamo*. New York: Palgrave Macmillan.

Langbein, John H. 1978. "Torture and Plea Bargaining." *University of Chicago Law Review* 46: 3–22.

——. 2006. *Torture and the Law of Proof: Europe and England in the Ancient Regime*. Chicago: University of Chicago Press.

Langguth, A.J. 1979. *Hidden Terrors: The Truth about US Police Operations in Latin America*. New York: Pantheon.

Lazreg, Marnia. 2008. *Torture and the Twilight of Empire: From Algiers to Baghdad*. Princeton, NJ: Princeton University Press.

Leopold, Jason. 2011. "Torture's Other Victims: US Soldiers." *Truthout*, (December 20). http://truth-out.org/index.php?option=com_k2&view=item&id=5360:tortures-other-victims-us-soldiers.

Lobe, Jim. 2011. "US Poll Tracks Shifts in Public Attitudes since 9/11." *Inter Press Service*, (September 1). http://ipsnews.net/print.asp?idnews=104965.

Luban, David J. 2005. "Liberalism, Torture, and the Ticking Bomb." *Virginia Law Review 91*: 1,425–61.

——. 2008. "Unthinking the Ticking Bomb." Georgetown Public Law Research Paper No. 1154202. http://papers.ssrn.com/sol3/papers.cfm?abstract_id=1154202.

Lutz, Ellen, and Caitlin Reiger, eds. 2009. *Prosecuting Heads of State*. New York: Cambridge University Press.

Mackey, Chris, and Greg Miller. 2004. *The Interrogators: Inside the Secret War against Al-Qaeda*. New York: Little, Brown.

MacNair, Rachel. 2002. *Perpetration-Induced Traumatic Stress: The Psychological Consequences of Killing*. Santa Barbara, CA: Praeger.

Mayer, Jane. 2005. "The Experiment." *New Yorker*, (July 11). http://www.newyorker.com/archive/2005/07/11/050711fa_fact4.

——. 2008. *The Dark Side: The Inside Story of How the War on Terror Turned into a War on American Ideals*. New York: Doubleday.

McCoy, Alfred. 2006. *A Question of Torture: CIA Interrogation, From the Cold War to the War on Terror*. New York: Metropolitan Books.

Menicucci, Garay. 2005. "Sexual Torture: Rendering, Practices, Manuals." *ISIM Review 16*: 18–19.

Miles, Steven H. 2006. *Oath Betrayed: Torture, Medical Complicity, and the War on Terror*. New York: Random House.

Morris, Errol. 2008. *Standard Operating Procedure* (film). Culver City, CA: Sony Pictures.

Nance, Malcolm. 2007. "Waterboarding Is Torture … Period." *Small Wars Journal*, (October 31). http://smallwarsjournal.com/blog/2007/10/waterboarding-is-torture-perio.

Neely, Brandon. 2008. *Testimony of Spc. Brandon Neely*. Guantánamo Testimonials Project, Center for the Study of Human Rights, University of California, Davis, (December 4). http://humanrights.ucdavis.edu/projects/the-Guantánamo-testimonialsproject/testimonies/testimonies-of-military-guards/testimony-of-brandon-neely.

Nielsen, Laura Beth. 2004. "The Work of Rights and the Work Rights Do: A Critical Empirical Approach." *The Blackwell Companion to Law and Society*, ed. Austin Sarat, Pp. 63–79 in. Boston: Blackwell.

Ortiz, Diane. 2002. *The Blindfold's Eyes: My Journey from Torture to Truth*. Maryknoll, NY: Orbis Books.

Orwell, George. 1949. *1984*. New York: Harcourt Brace Jovanovich.

Osiel, Mark. 2004. "The Mental State of Torturers: Argentina's Dirty War." *Torture: A Collection*, ed. Sanford Levinson, Pp. 129–41 in. New York: Oxford University Press.

Parry, John. 2003. "What Is Torture, Are We Doing It, and What If We Are?" *University of Pittsburgh Law Review 64*: 237–62.

PCATI (Public Committee against Torture in Israel). 2003. *Back to a Routine of Torture: Torture and Ill-treatment of Palestinian Detainees during Arrest, Detention and Interrogation*. Jerusalem.

Pereira, Anthony W. 2008. "Of Judges and Generals: Security Courts under Authoritarian Regimes in Argentina, Brazil, and Chile." *Rule by Law: The Politics of Courts in Authoritarian Regimes*, eds. Tom Ginsberg and Tamir Moustafa, Pp. 23–57 in. New York: Cambridge University Press.

Peters, Edward. 1996. *Torture*. Philadelphia: University of Pennsylvania Press.

Phillips, Joshua E. S. 2010. *None of Us Were Like This Before: American Soldiers and Torture*. New York: Verso.

Polanski, Roman. 1994. *Death and the Maiden* (film). New York: Fine Line Features.

Pontecorvo, Gillo. 1966. *The Battle of Algiers* (film). Algiers/Rome: Casbah Films, Igor Film.

Priest, Dana. 2005. "CIA Holds Terror Suspects in Secret Prisons." *Washington Post*, (November 2). http://www.washingtonpost.com/wp-dyn/content/article/2005/11/01/AR2005110101644.html.

Priest, Dana, and Barton Gellman. 2002. "US Decries Abuse But Defends Interrogations: 'Stress and Duress' Tactics Used on Terrorism Suspects Held in Secret Overseas Facilities." *Washington Post* (December 26): A1, A14–15.

Ratner, Michael, and Center for Constitutional Rights. 2008. *The Trial of Donald Rumsfeld: A Prosecution by the Book*. New York: New Press.

Rejali, Darius. 2007. *Torture and Democracy*. Princeton, NJ: Princeton University Press.

Ron, James. 1997. "Varying Methods of State Violence." *International Organizations 51*: 275–300.

Ron, James. 2003. *Frontiers and Ghettos: State Violence in Serbia and Israel*. Berkeley: University of California Press.

Rose, David. 2004a. "Operation Take Away My Freedom: Inside Guantánamo Bay on Trial." *Vanity Fair*, (January). http://www.vanityfair.com/politics/features/2004/01/Guantánamo200401.

——. 2004b. *Guantánamo: The War on Human Rights*. New York: New Press.

——. 2008. "Tortured Reasoning." *Vanity Fair*, (December 16) (web edition). http://www.vanityfair.com/magazine/2008/12/torture200812.

Rosenberg, Gerald N. 1991. *The Hollow Hope: Can Courts Bring about Social Change?* Chicago: University of Chicago Press.

Saar, Erik, and Viveca Novak. 2005. *Inside the Wire: A Military Intelligence Soldier's Eyewitness Account of Life at Guantánamo*. New York: Penguin.

Sands, Philip. 2008. *Torture Team: Rumsfeld's Memo and the Betrayal of American Values*. Hampshire, UK: Palgrave Macmillan.

Scarry, Elaine. 1985. *The Body in Pain: The Making and Unmaking of the World*. New York: Oxford University Press.

Scheppele, Kim. 2005. "Hypothetical Torture in the 'War on Terrorism.'" *Journal of National Security Policy and Law 1*: 285–340.

Scheingold, Stuart. 2004. *The Politics of Rights: Lawyers, Public Policy, and Political Change*, 2nd edition. Ann Arbor, MI: University of Michigan Press.

Sharrock, Justine. 2008. "Am I a Torturer?" *Mother Jones*, (March 3). http://www.motherjones.com/politics/2008/03/am-i-torturer.

Shue, Henry. 2004. "Torture." *Torture: A Collection*, ed. Sanford Levinson, Pp. 47–60 in. New York: Oxford University Press.

Simon, Jonathan. 1998. "Discipline and Punish: The Birth of a Post-Modern Middle-Range." *Required Reading: Sociology's Most Influential Texts*, ed. D. Clawson, Pp. 47–54 in. Boston: University of Massachusetts Press.

Soldz, Stephen, and Brad Olson. 2008. "Psychologists, Detainee Interrogations, and Torture: Varying Perspectives on Nonparticipation." *The Trauma of Psychological Torture*, ed. A.E. Ojeda, Pp. 70–91 in. Westport, CT: Praeger.

Soufan, Ali. 2009. "My Tortured Decision." *New York Times*, (Apr. 23). http://www.nytimes.com/2009/04/23/opinion/23soufan.html.

—— with Daniel Freedman. 2011. *The Black Banners: The Inside Story of 9/11 and the War against Al-Qaeda.* New York: W.W. Norton and Co.

Suskind, Ron. 2006. *The One Percent Doctrine: Deep inside America's Pursuit of Its Enemies since 9/11.* New York: Simon & Schuster.

Swenson, Russell, ed. 2006. *Educing Information: Interrogation: Science and Art, Intelligence Science Board, Phase 1 Report.* Washington, DC: National Defense Intelligence College. http://www.fas.org/irp/dni/educing.pdf.

Taguba, Antonio. 2004. Taguba Report: Article 15–6 Investigation of the 800th Military Police Brigade. Washington, DC: Department of Defense. Reproduced in *The Torture Papers: The Road to Abu Ghraib*, 2005, eds. K. J. Greenberg and J. L. Dratel, pp. 405–555.

——. 2008. "Preface." In *Broken Laws, Broken Lives: Medical Evidence of Torture by the US.* Physicians for Human Rights. http://brokenlives.info/?page_id=23.

Taussig, Michael. 1984. "Culture of Terror—Space of Death: Roger Casement's Putumayo Report and the Explanation for Torture." *Comparative Studies in Society and History 26*: 479–84.

Thornhill, Theresa. 1992. *Making Women Talk: The Interrogation of Palestinian Women Detainees.* London: Lawyers for Palestinian Human Rights.

Timerman, Jacobo. 1981. *Prisoner Without a Name, Cell Without a Number.* New York: Knopf.

Turner, Bryan. 1993. "Outline of a Theory of Human Rights." *Sociology 27*: 489–512.

——. 2006. *Vulnerability and Human Rights.* University Park: Pennsylvania State University Press.

Umansky, Eric. 2008. "Six Gitmo Prosecutors Who Protested." *ProPublica*, (October 1). http://www.propublica.org/article/the-six-gitmo-prosecutors-who-protested-1001.

US Senate Armed Services Committee. 2008. *Investigation into the Treatment of Detainees in US Custody: Executive Summary and Conclusions.* Washington, DC: US Senate. http://levin.senate.gov/newsroom/supporting/2008/Detainees.121108.pdf.

Walsh, James I., and James A. Piazza. 2010. "Why Respecting Physical Integrity Rights Reduces Terrorism." *Comparative Political Studies 43*: 551–77.

Walsh, Joan, ed. 2003. "The Abu Ghraib Files." *Salon.com.* http://www.salon.com/2006/03/14/introduction_2.

Weschler, Lawrence. 1998. *A Miracle, A Universe: Settling Accounts with Torturers.* Chicago: University of Chicago Press.

Williams, Patricia J. 1991. *The Alchemy of Race and Rights: Diary of a Law Professor.* Cambridge: Harvard University Press.

Worthington, Andy. 2007. *The Guantánamo Files: The Stories of the 759 Detainees in America's Illegal Prison.* London: Pluto.

Zimbardo, Phillip G. 2007. *The Lucifer Effect: Understanding How Good People Turn Evil.* New York: Random House.

Glossary/Index

~~~

Page numbers followed by 'f' refer to figures.

1984 23, 61
24 2

A

abolition of torture: when judicial torture was expunged from legal systems as a lawful procedure to investigate crimes 19–20

Abrahamian, Ervand 22

Abu Ghraib: a prison in Baghdad, Iraq, that became infamous in 2004 as a site where US abuse and torture of prisoners was "systematic" and "wanton" 7, 48, 58, 59

    photos 7–8, 7f, 52–53, 53f

    sexualized humiliation and torture in 52–53

    Taguba report on 7

    talking about torture after photos 9–10

Abu Zubaydah 9, 48, 56, 57

actionable intelligence: forward-looking information of national security value 6, 9, 54, 57

al-Libi, Ibn al-Shaykh 58

al-Qaeda 9, 54, 57, 58, 59, 60

al-Qahtani, Muhammad 58

Algeria 24

Améry, Jean 51

Amnesty International 6, 41

Ancient Greece 14–15

anti-torture deontologists: people who oppose torture under all circumstances because it is illegal and immoral 4

antiquity, torture in 14–16

Arab-Israeli War 30

Arendt, Hannah 23, 54

Argentina 28

authoritarianism: when state power is concentrated in the hands of a few political leaders and repression is frequently used to maintain that power. Authoritarian regimes can include military juntas, fascist or racist regimes, dictatorships, theocracies, and one-party states. What they have in common is an utter lack of accountability of the state to society 23

B
black sites: secret overseas prisons run by the CIA 9, 12, 48, 49
Blackstone, William 18
brainwashing 25, 27
Brazil 28, 54, 55
Bumiller, Kristin 35
Bush administration 9, 10, 11, 57
    reaction to Abu Ghraib photos 7–8
Bush, President George W. 5, 8, 11, 45, 47, 49

C
Calling the Ghosts 52
Cambodia 23
Central Intelligence Agency (CIA)
    to adhere to same rules as military 12
    concerns over vulnerability to prosecution 9
    "exception" 10
    interrogations and detentions 9, 11, 48, 49, 56, 57, 58
    mind-control research 25–26, 27
    Phoenix program 26, 27
    subject to universal jurisdiction 48, 49
Cheney, Dick 2, 12, 56, 57, 58
Chicago Boys 27
Chile 27–28, 46–47, 51–52
China 22, 25
Christians 16
civil war: armed conflict within a country, usually pitting a government against one or more opposition groups 22
    see also **conventional war; unconventional/aysmmetric war**
Clinton, President Bill 45
Cohen, Stanley 42
Cold War 25–26, 44
colonialism: when one country claims sovereignty over a conquered foreign territory and its population, and establishes a colony. The history of colonialism dates back to the 1500s when European governments began taking over and

establishing colonial rule throughout the Americas, Africa, and Asia 23–24, 26

Common Article 3: common to the four Geneva Conventions of 1949, this article pertains to the treatment of combatants or civilians who are captured in "non-international" (i.e. not state-to-state) wars and conflicts 11

confessions: first- or third-person accounts of criminal wrongdoing 15

Medieval 16–17, 18

modern tortured 22, 52, 57

of Palestinian detainees 30

consequentialism 3

Convention against Torture and Other Cruel, Inhuman or Degrading Treatment or Punishment (CAT): a human rights law passed by the United Nations in 1984 that pertains specifically to the international legal rights of people in custody 8, 39

conventional war: armed conflict between or among states and their militaries 22
see also **civil war; unconventional/asymmetric war**

core crimes under international law: torture, war crimes, genocide and crimes against humanity, which constitute the most serious class of violations 41, 44, 46, 47

costs of US torture, indirect 12–13, 57, 59, 60

"counter resistance" techniques for military interrogators 54–55

courts, challenging torture in 10–12, 45–46

Crenshaw, Kimberle 35

crimes against humanity: large-scale and/or systematic attacks on civilians and civilian infrastructure, whether occurring in war or peace 37, 40

Critical Race Theory 35

critique of the critique of rights 35

crucifixion 15–16

cruel, inhumane and degrading treatment: similar to torture, but a category of practices deemed relatively less awful 10, 29, 40

Cuba 26

D

Danner, Mark 51, 53, 55

Dayan, Colin 19–20

de-legitimization of torture: political unacceptability of torture because it violates rights and dignity of human beings and is an unacceptable exercise of state power 19–20

Death and the Maiden 51–52

Decision Points 49

democracy: a government that represents society and in which members of society—at least citizens—have an institutionalized opportunity to pick and change their political leaders through elections and other lawful and peaceful means 24–25

torture in a 29–32

deontology 4

Dershowitz, Alan 3–4

Detainee Treatment Act 2005 11

Dirani, Mustafa 52

disappeared, to be: a form of extra-judicial execution where the victim's body is destroyed or hidden 28

domestic violence 34

Dorfman, Ariel 47, 51

DuBois, Paige 15

E

Egypt 6, 52, 58

Eighth Amendment to the US Constitution (1791): part of US Bill of Rights; prohibits the government from imposing excessive bail, excessive fines, and cruel and unusual punishments 19–20

El-Masri, Khaled 49

electric torture 24

English law 18

enhanced interrogation techniques: American euphemism for officially authorized torture techniques and cruel, inhuman, and degrading treatment of prisoners captured in the war on terror 10, 43, 49, 56

Enlightenment thought: broadly understood as a modernizing trend during the 17th and 18th centuries that stressed intellectual reason, logic, criticism, and freedom of thought and disparaged political tyranny, superstition, and religious dogma 19–20

European Court of Human Rights (ECHR) 29, 31, 49

extra-judicial execution: killing individuals for political reasons, and without authorization by a court of law 23, 26

extraordinary rendition: kidnapping/arrest and secret transfer by the CIA to a foreign country for the purpose of interrogation 6, 48

F

Feldman, Allen 29, 53

Formations of Violence 53

Foucault, Michel 14, 17, 19, 33

frail human body 40

France 24, 48–49

Frankenheimer, John 25

Friedman, Milton 27

G

Garzón, Baltazar 46, 49

Gellman, Barton 6

General Security Service (GSS) 30

Geneva Convention 1864 38

Geneva Convention 1929 38

Geneva Conventions, 1949: the main body of international humanitarian law which
composes part of the laws of war 8, 11, 38, 47

Geneva Protocol 1925 38

genocide: a crime that is defined as "acts committed with intent to destroy, in whole
or in part, a national, ethnical, racial or religious group, as such" 38, 41
attempt to broaden definition of 46–47
in Rwanda and Yugoslavia 44–45, 45f

Genocide Convention: passed by the United Nations in 1948; the first human rights law 38

Germany 48, 49
Nazi xii, 23, 25, 36–37, 38

Goering, Hermann 36–37

Gonzales, Alberto 8

Great Britain
arrest of Pinochet in 46–47
interrogation of IRA 29, 31, 53

Greenberg, Karen 4, 5, 9

Guantánamo: a US naval base on the south side of the island of Cuba, selected in
December 2001 as the main site to interrogate and detain "unlawful combatants"
captured in the war on terror 5–6, 8, 9, 11, 54, 58
foreign criminal indictments regarding torture at 48, 49
initiatives to close 12
inspiring recruitment of foreign fighters to Iraq 59
numbers of detainees released from 12
Red Cross on 55

H

habeas corpus: also referred to as The Great Writ, a customary law imperative for any
government to legally justify why a person is being detained. Purpose is to prohibit
the imprisonment of people without just cause 5, 19

Hajjar, Lisa 30, 47, 49

Hamdan v. Rumsfeld 2006 11

heresy 16, 17, 18

high-value detainees (HVDs): individuals suspected by the US government of
being leaders or planners of terrorist attacks or having knowledge about terrorist
plots and networks 9, 11, 48, 56, 57, 58

history of torture 14–20
    in antiquity 14–16
    invention of 14
    legal abolition of judicial 19–20
    in medieval Europe 16–18
Holocaust 36–37, 38
Horton, Scott 9, 49, 56, 58, 59
Huggins, Martha 54
human rights: rights that apply to all human beings (i.e. universal) and are indivisible (i.e. all humans have all human rights) 33
    creation of 36–39
    understanding right not to be tortured 39–40
human rights activism: strategies (i.e. monitoring, reporting, advocacy, litigation) intended to close the "gap" between laws in the books and law in action 41–42
human rights law: international treaties that provide humans' right to rights. Originated in 1948 with the Universal Declaration of Human Rights and the Genocide Convention 8, 38, 39, 42
human rights movement: the globalized panoply of organizations and activities motivated by a common goal of closing the gap between international human rights laws in the books and law in action 41–42
human rights organizations: institutions with explicit human rights mandates 41–42
Human Rights Watch 6, 42, 48, 49, 52
humanitarianism: caring about the suffering of "strangers" because of a sense of shared humanity, and acting in ways intended to alleviate that suffering 19
hypothetical ticking bomb scenario: an imaginary scenario in which a bomb is set to explode and the lives of hundreds, thousands, or even millions of people are at risk (depending on the nature and location of this hypothetical bomb). The person who knows where the bomb is and how to defuse it has been captured but he or she is refusing to divulge this information 3, 4–5, 32

I

implicatory denial: when a government admits that wrongdoing occurred but blames it on (i.e. implicates) rogues who allegedly broke rather than followed rules and policies 7–8, 43
    see also **interpretative denial**; **literal denial**; **politics of denial**
Indochina 24
International Committee of the Red Cross 55
International Covenant on Civil and Political Rights (ICCPR) 39
International Covenant on Economic, Social and Cultural Rights (ICESCR) 39

International Criminal Court (ICC): international (UN-created) court to prosecute individuals accused of core crimes under international law (torture, genocide, war crimes, and crimes against humanity). Was established in 2002 and is based in The Hague 45–46

international criminal law: the body of international law that makes torture, war crimes, genocide, and crimes against humanity prosecutable offenses 44–46, 46–47

international humanitarian law (IHL): a set of rules that seeks to limit unnecessary human suffering in war and armed conflict 8, 39

    see also **Geneva Conventions, 1949**

interpretative denial: if the evidence of wrongdoing is too clear or well substantiated to be denied with literal lies, or if a government wants to avoid the consequences without actually altering its tactics, officials use euphemisms to insist that what was authorized was not the bad thing (e.g. torture) but something else, like "moderate physical pressure" or "enhanced interrogation methods" 43

    see also **implacatory denial**; **literal denial**; **politics of denial**

interrogational torture: to extract actionable intelligence, particularly in the context of war or conflict 22–23, 26, 32

    see also **terroristic torture**

invention of torture 14

Iran 22

Iraq 7, 57–58, 59

Ireland 29

Ireland v. *United Kingdom* 29

Irish Republican Army (IRA) 29, 31, 53

Israel 29–32, 52

Italian courts 48

J

Jackson, US Supreme Court Justice Robert 37

judicial torture: painful questioning to extract a confession or other information for a legal process 14, 15, 16–17, 19, 22

    see also **penal torture**

K

Khalid Sheikh Muhammad (KSM) 11, 57

Kimmitt, Brigadier General Mark 7

Klein, Naomi 27, 28

Korean War 25

Kubark Counterintelligence Interrogation 26

L

Landau Commission 30–31, 32

Langbein, John 14, 17–18, 19

Latin America 26–27, 27–29, 44, 47

legacy of US torture 12–13, 59, 60

Levin, Carl 56

literal denial: when officials refute allegations or evidence of wrongdoing with false proclamations that "we don't do that" 42

see also **implacatory denial**; **interpretative denial**; **politics of denial**

Luban, David 19, 56

M

Mackey, Chris 54

MacNair, Rachel 59

McCain, John 10, 12

McCoy, Alfred 26, 55

medieval Europe, torture in 16–18

Military Commissions Act (MCA), 2006, 2009: following the Supreme Court's 2006 decision in *Hamdan* v. *Rumsfeld* which declared the presidentially created military commission system unconstitutional, Congress passed this Act to re-establish it. The Act was revised in 2009 11

military commissions (US): on November 13, 2001, President George W. Bush issued a military order which included the establishment of special military courts to try foreign terror suspects. The military commissions are based at Guantánamo 11, 58

mind-control research 25–26, 27

MK-ULTRA program 25

moderate physical pressure: Israeli euphemism for officially authorized torture techniques and cruel and degrading treatment of Palestinian prisoners 31, 32

Mora, Alberto 12–13, 59

N

Nasr, Hassan Mustafa Osama 48

nation-state: a state that governs a specific nation of people and the territory in which they live 21

National Security Strategy 2005 11

national security: the right of a state to defend and preserve itself and the duty to protect society 21–22, 28

Nazi Germany xii, 23, 25, 36–37, 38

negative rights: freedom from something that is legally prohibited 34

see also **positive rights**; **rights**

New York Times 56

Niemöller, Pastor Martin xii

None of Us Were Like This Before 59

North Korea 25

Northern Ireland 29, 31, 53

Nowak, Manfred 42

Nuremberg and Tokyo Tribunals: special courts established at the end of World War II to prosecute leaders of the defeated nations of Germany and Japan for serious crimes 36–37, 44

O

Obama, President Barack 12, 13, 58

Office of Legal Counsel (OLC): section of the US Justice Department that functions as "the government's lawyer," including providing advice about the legality of government policies 8, 9, 10

Omar, Abu 48

Orwell, George 23, 61

Osiel, Mark 54

P

Palestine 29–32

paradox of pre-modern torture: in pre-modern societies where torture was a feature of legal procedures, it was both necessary to enforce the law and regarded as dubious for eliciting truthful statements 18

paradox of torture: the fact that torture is both absolutely illegal and pervasive around the globe 42–43

pathological effects of torture on perpetrating institutions and societies 55

penal torture: physically painful or excruciating forms of punishment 14, 19

 see also **judicial torture**

perpetrators, effects of torture on 53–55

Peters, Edward 14, 15, 21

Phillips, Joshua 59

physicians involved in torture 55

Piazza, James 60

Pinochet, Augusto 27–28, 29, 46–47

Pinochet precedent: the outcome of a decision by the British Law Lords in 1999 that even a former head of state (Augusto Pinochet) could be extradited to a foreign country and prosecuted for torture under the doctrine of universal jurisdiction because there is no sovereign immunity for torture 47

politics of denial: as used here, when government officials accused of engaging in or abetting very serious crimes are politically compelled to deny their wrongdoing in order to defend their reputations and avoid consequences 42

 see also **implicatory denial; interpretative denial; literal denial**

positive rights: freedom to something that the state is legally obligated to provide or do 33

see also **negative rights**; **rights**

post-traumatic stress disorder (PTSD) 59

presumption of innocence 19

Priest, Dan 6, 48

prisoners, contemporary treatment of 20

prisoners of war (POWs): captured soldiers from another/enemy country 25

pro-torture consequentialists: people who argue that under certain exceptional circumstances torture might be necessary to save innocent lives and, thus, under those circumstances it is legitimate. Consequentialism is a class of ethical theory which holds that the morality of conduct should be judged on the basis of its outcome or consequences 3, 4, 12, 56, 57, 60

Project X 26–27

prosecutions against suspected terrorists, US 58

psychological torture: tactics that target the mind, although they may involve physical methods, such as those that fuse sensory deprivation and stress positions 26

psychologists 55, 57

public debates on torture 3, 5, 6–7, 40

public opinion on torture 6, 10

in French war with Algeria 24

public opinion polls 2

punishment 36

R

rape 45, 52

Rasul v. *Bush* 2004 11

regime type: a form of government and the social organization of a political system 23–25

see also **authoritarianism**; **colonialism**; **democracy**; **totalitarianism**

Rejali, Darius 24, 55, 60

rights: legal entitlements constituted through practices that are required, prohibited, or otherwise regulated through relations governed by law 33

and core international crimes 40–41

creation of Human Rights 36–39

critique of the critique of rights 35

human right not to be tortured 39–40

human rights activism 41–42

importance of having 34–36

and paradox of torture *see* **paradox of torture**

understanding 33–34

see also **negative rights; positive rights**

Roman Empire: a vast political system dominated by rulers (emperors) based in Rome, at its peak extending from northern Europe to North Africa and the eastern Mediterranean. Imperial government was complex and bureaucratic, characterized by a mix of autocratic rule, separation of powers, and political rights for some classes of citizens 16

Roman law: the legal system of ancient Rome and the empire. Characteristics included professional jurists, and the treatment of law as a kind of science. Influenced the development of legal systems in medieval Europe and some other parts of the world 15–16, 17, 59–60

Ron, James 22, 54

Rose, David 6, 8, 56, 57

Rumsfeld, Donald 7, 9, 11, 12
    efforts to indict 48–49

Rwanda 44, 45f, 46

S

Scheingold, Stuart 35

Scheppele, Kim 4–5, 56

School of the Americas (US Army): established in Panama in 1946 to train military officials from allied countries in South and Central America in counter-insurgency warfare and to indoctrinate them about the dangers of communism. In 2001, it was renamed the Western Hemisphere Institute for Security Cooperation 26, 27

self-determination: the right of a people (usually conceived as a nation) to rule themselves and to have a sovereign state of their own 24

sensory deprivation: deliberate reduction or removal of stimuli from one or more of the senses (sound, sight, light, etc.). Over prolonged periods this can cause extreme anxiety, depression, hallucinations, and suicidal thoughts 5, 26

September 11, 2001; also 9/11: date of devastating terrorist attacks on the US by al-Qaeda operatives who hijacked airplanes that were crashed into the World Trade Center Towers in New York City, the Pentagon in Washington, DC, and one that was destined for another target but was diverted by passengers and crashed in Pennsylvania 1
    changing views in US on torture after 2–5

sexualized torture 52–53

Shue, Henry 23

slave torture 15

slaves, violence against 19

socialism 39

Soufan, Ali 56–57

South Korea 25

sovereignty: typically describes the power and authority of states. In the international system, sovereign states are equals (at least in principle) 21

Soviet Union (USSR) 25, 26

Spain 49

Spee, Friedrich von 60

state secrets privilege (US): a doctrine that allows the government to withhold sensitive pieces of information if it is in the country's national security interest to do so 11

state terror 23
  in Latin America 27–29

states' rights: to be independent (political autonomy), to rule over a specific territory and population (domestic jurisdiction), and to be free from outside intervention by other states (non-interference) 21

stress positions: positioning and immobilizing a person's body in such a way that a great amount of weight is placed on just one or two muscles 5, 31

suicide bombing 32, 59

Supreme Court (US): the country's highest court whose authority includes ruling on the constitutionality and legality of government actions and policies 11

Switzerland 49

T

Taguba, Antonio 13

Taguba Report (2004) 7

terroristic torture: rampant custodial violence in the context of state terror, often coupled with extra-judicial execution 23, 26, 28
  see also **interrogational torture**

The Black Banners 57–58

The Manchurian Candidate 25

torture: purposefully causing a person who is in custody to experience severe physical and/or mental pain and suffering 1
  after Abu Ghraib 9–10
  changing views in US after 9/11 2–5
  Court challenges in US to 10–12
  how US became a regime using 8–9
  ineffectiveness of 4, 9, 11–12, 24, 26, 28, 55–58
  information on treatment of prisoners in US custody 5–8
  legacy of US 12–13, 59, 60
  modern purposes of 22–23
  speaking out against 10, 12–13

see also **delegitimization of torture; interrogational torture; judicial torture; penal torture; psychological torture; terroristic torture**

torture lite: a euphemism for tactics that do not permanently damage or destroy the body 3–4

torture memos: descriptive term for legal memoranda produced by government lawyers and policy documents pertaining to the interrogation and detention of prisoners captured in the war on terror that reveal how the Bush administration sought to evade the prohibition of torture by reinterpreting the law 7, 8, 9, 20, 32

totalitarianism: a political system in which the state exercises total power over all aspects of society, and state terror is pervasive. The Soviet Union during Stalin's era and Nazi Germany are the archetypal models of totalitarian states 23

trials by ordeal: early pre-modern forms of painful or even deadly processes to which people accused of committing crimes were subjected. The presumption was that the outcomes (survival or death) would reflect God's truth 16

truth and torture 15, 17, 18, 56, 59–60

U

Ulpian 59–60

unconventional/asymmetric war: armed conflict between states and non-state groups 22

see also **civil war; conventional war**

United Nations (UN): an international organization established in 1945 whose membership is composed of representatives of states. Mandate was defined in the UN Charter to provide a forum for meeting and collaboration to ensure the common good of global peace and security. Among its functions, the UN is the institution where international law is made 37, 39

ad hoc tribunals 44–45, 46, 52

Universal Declaration of Human Rights (UDHR): a document passed by the UN in 1948 to establish "a common standard of achievement for all peoples and all nations," which laid out a framework for a common and collective ("universal" and "indivisible") set of rights that all humans could claim. Although the UDHR is not a law, it served as a reference for subsequent efforts to transform those principles into actual international laws 37

universal jurisdiction: a distinctive method of criminal accountability which permits individuals accused of very serious international crimes to be prosecuted in a foreign national legal system even if that country has no connection to the crime on the principle that some crimes are so egregious that perpetrators should find no sanctuary. Originated in the 19th century to close jurisdictional gaps in order to prosecute pirates and slave traders, whose crimes occurred largely on the high seas. The Pinochet precedent gave this a new purpose at the end of the 20th century to enable prosecution of individuals for torture and other core crimes 46–47

US torture and 47–49

unlawful combatants: refers to people who are neither lawful combatants (i.e. soldiers) nor civilians and who actively participate in armed conflict or otherwise violate the laws of war. International law experts regard such people as civilians (under IHL civilians have no "right to fight" except under very limited circumstances) but the Bush administration devised this concept to exclude captured enemies and suspects from either category 5, 6, 11

Uruguay 28

V

victims of torture 51–53

Vietnam 26

Violence Workers 54

W

Walsh, Joan 7

Walsh, John 60

war: armed conflict 5

see also **civil war**; **conventional war**; **unconventional/assymetric war**

war crimes: serious violations (also referred to as grave breaches) of the Geneva Conventions and other laws of war 13, 38, 41

rape classified as a 45, 52

war on terror: a global military and political campaign led by the US and initiated in response to the 9/11 terrorist attacks. Main targets are terrorists and Islamist militants and governments that assist them 1, 2, 10, 55, 60

justification to expand 57–58

rights of detainees in 5

US decides Geneva conventions do not apply in 8, 47

Washington Post 6, 48

waterboarding: a torture tactic to induce the feeling and fear of death by drowning 9, 10, 11, 13, 49, 57

Weschler, Lawrence 28

witchery 17

World War One 38

World War Two 36–37

Y

Yugoslavia 44, 45f, 52

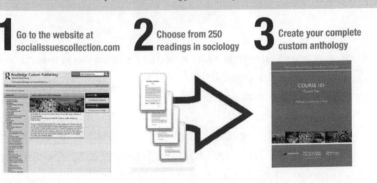